Touch

An Exploration

NORMAN AUTTON

Darton, Longman and Todd
London

First published in 1989 by
Darton, Longman and Todd Ltd
89 Lillie Road, London SW6 1UD

© 1989 Norman Autton

The diagrams on pages 81 and 82 are reproduced from
J. J. Lynch, *The Broken Heart: The Medical Consequences
of Loneliness* (1977) by permission of Basic Books, New York.

British Library Cataloguing in Publication Data

Autton, Norman
  Touch.
  1. Mental healing. Use of touch
  I. Title
  615.8'51

  ISBN 0–232–51822–X

Phototypeset by Input Typesetting Ltd
London SW19 8DR
Printed and bound in Great Britain by
Courier International Ltd
Tiptree, Essex

To
KATE
with gratitude

Contents

Preface   ix

Prologue   1

1 Nature of Touch   3

2 Touch in the Development of the Life Cycle   23

3 Touch in the Care of the Sick   40

4 Touch in Stress and Crisis Situations   63

5 Touch in Counselling and Psychotherapy   89

6 Touch in the Care of the Aged, the Dying and the
   Bereaved   108

7 Healing Touch   129

Epilogue   144

Index of Proper Names   147

General Index   151

Preface

This present study has been undertaken to serve as a companion volume to *Pain: An Exploration* (Darton, Longman and Todd 1986). Asexual touch has been a somewhat neglected sphere of pastoral care, and the following pages are an attempt to explore its use and significance in various aspects of caring and healing. Unfortunately physical touch has become rather formalized and associated with sexual connotation. It is normally seen as either sexual, violent or medical with little or no emphasis placed on its healing potential. As one professor comments, 'We are such a sexually orientated culture that the therapeutic effect of asexual touch has been neglected. . . . It is perhaps rather sad you have to be old and dying before the doctor can hold your hand without the contact being open to misinterpretation!'

It is surprising that physical touch, a powerful and nonverbal stimulus, particularly in times of anxiety, fear and distress, has rarely been studied within a pastoral context. Indeed it seems to have received much less scientific attention than either sight or hearing. Neisser (1966) notes how:

> special journals are devoted to optics and to acoustics, to research in vision and to disorders of hearing; entire laboratories specialize in psycho-acoustics or in visual research. Nobel Prizes have been awarded for the discovery of basic mechanisms in both modalities. Touch has far less glamour and prestige, and we know correspondingly less about it.

In our society there appears to be an unwritten touch-me-not policy for all except intimate friends. We tend to slight an important aspect of our physical and emotional constitution, for as Aristotle argued (*On the Soul*, 434b), physical touch is the most fundamental of all the five senses. Characteristic of our contemporary culture is a drift towards minimizing personal encounter.

This book has been written to explore the use of asexual touch in inter-personal relationships from the first days of birth to the final stages of life. It is to be hoped that in the chapters which follow, priests and ministers (especially those serving as hospital chaplains), members of the medical and nursing professions, social workers and all professional carers, will find helpful information and guidance as to the use of touch to foster meaningful relationships and to offer comfort, security and healing to all who are in need, be that need physical, emotional, mental or spiritual.

A number of friends and colleagues have helped to contribute to the writing of the book and have stimulated my own thinking on the various aspects of touch outlined in its pages. As the reader will note from the Prologue I was privileged to spend time at l'Arche with Jean Vanier and members of the staff and helpers, in the community at Trosly-Breuil. They taught me much about how the lives of those who are mentally handicapped can be enriched by touch – a touch which confirms their 'loveable-ness', gives them a sense of belonging and grants them an inner peace. Dr Thérèse Vanier, who has recently retired from her work at St Christopher's Hospice, London, willingly shared some of her experiences of working both with the mentally handicapped and the terminally ill. Henri Nouwen, author of much valued works on the caring ministry and the spiritual life, generously devoted time in the midst of his 'journeyings oft', to discuss a number of major issues involved in the use of touch.

On the general theme of touch Mrs Jean Lugton, Judith Ashton and Dr Robin Hull, Macmillan Senior Lecturer in Palliative Care, Medical School, Birmingham, offered most constructive viewpoints. Dr Inge B. Corless, Chairman of Secondary Care Dept., University of North Carolina, USA, also freely shared helpful information.

For the subjects dealt with in Chapters 2 and 4 of the book Dr Marshall H. Klaus, Professor of Paediatrics, University of California, USA, very generously shared some of his own thinking and research on problems concerning premature and very sick infants, and the importance of mother-child relationships. Senior nursing staff of the premature baby units at Hammersmith Hospital, London, and Wycombe General Hospital, High Wycombe, Bucks, most thoughtfully contributed from their own personal experiences of nursing very sick babies and of caring for the parents and families. Dr J. Hopkins of Johnson & Johnson Ltd., forwarded much useful material. Dr Mark Drayton, Consultant Paediatrician, University Hospital of Wales, Cardiff, was also generous enough to read the above chapters and offered constructive comments.

I am most grateful to the staff of a number of hospices and to leading international authorities in the care of the terminally ill and bereaved for their contributions to Chapter 6. St Luke's Nursing Home, Sheffield, St Mary's Hospice, Birmingham, and St David's Foundation, Newport, Gwent, arranged multi-disciplinary discussion groups and reported back some of their findings on the use and significance of physical touch with the dying and their families. Individual contributions were also received from Dr E. Kubler-Ross, Virginia, USA; Mother Frances Dominica, Helen House, Oxford; Professor Ivan Lichter, Te Omanga Hospice, New Zealand; Dr Robert Twycross, Sir Michael Sobell House, The Churchill Hospital, Oxford; Professor Eric Wilkes, Co-Chairman, Help the Hospices; Dr Colin Murray Parkes, The London Hospital Medical College; Professor John Hinton, St Christopher's Hospice, London, and Dr Derek Doyle, St Columba's Hospice, Edinburgh.

There are many others, too numerous to mention, who most readily shared their insights on the theme of touch, to all of whom I extend my sincere gratitude and appreciation.

For the sake of convenience and style, the male gender is used passim in the following pages. No sex discrimination is intended for the male pronoun is frequently used as a generic form.

Mr Cliff Morgan, Director of Nurse Education, University Hospital of Wales, and Jacqueline Beese, District Nurse Lecturer, University of Wales College of Medicine, generously arranged for a questionnaire on the use of touch in nursing to be circulated among their students: the librarians of the University of Wales College of Medicine, the School of Nursing Library at the Combined Training Institute, and the

Dental School Library, were always ready to procure books, journals and articles relevant to the study: Teresa de Bertodano, Editor, Darton, Longman and Todd, generously undertook the most time-consuming task of translating from the French some of the writings of Père Thomas Philippe, OP, which deal with the subject of touch.

My secretary, Mrs Anne Taylor, typed the manuscript through its various drafts with a most professional 'touch' and I am much indebted to her for her loyalty and her efficiency.

University Hospital of Wales, Cardiff   NORMAN AUTTON
29 September 1988
(St Michael and All Angels)

Neisser, U.   *Cognition and Reality Principles and Implications of Cognitive Psychology*. Freeman, San Francisco 1966.

Prologue

The universal language of touch was brought home to me during a recent stay at l'Arche, the Christian community for mentally handicapped adults in France. In the peace and tranquillity of the quiet French village of Trosly-Breuil, one hour's journey north of Paris, where the members of the community live, sections of this book came to be written.

L'Arche, founded by Jean Vanier some twenty-four years ago, now attracts staff and visitors from all over the world – the USA, Canada, Belgium, Syria, Poland, India, Italy, Holland and countless other lands. Many were unable to speak English: I was unable to speak French. The only way some of us were able to communicate was by gestures. Hands were waved, clasped, clutched, held and shaken. Often as we walked together we touched: often as we spoke together we touched.

Members of staff, helpers, guests, many of whom had academic backgrounds, gifted in their respective spheres of study and research, communicated freely with the mentally and physically handicapped, some of whom were blind and speechless, yet also gifted in their respective spheres of trust, simplicity, love and devotion, united in the common bond of touch.

At the Eucharist in the community chapel a number of the handicapped residents served at the altar, attentive and devout, dressed in their spotless albs, and proud to be able to touch the sacred vessels and attend the priests at the altar. We exchanged the 'Pax' in symbolic gesture: we often sang one of their favourite hymns, *Les Mains de Dieu* (The Hands of God):

1

Les mains de Dieu se sont posées
sur nos visages de misère,
les mains de Dieu ont caréssé nos coeurs meurtris
pour apaiser enfin le feu de nos douleurs.
*Poserons-nous ainsi nos mains?**

Poles, Dutch, Canadian, French, handicapped and non-handicapped, held hands together to sing 'grace' before and after meals. We greeted each other as brothers and sisters, living together in an atmosphere of security, in a life of true fellowship, peace and celebration. It was only language that created barriers; it was touch that knew no bounds. Handicapped and non-handicapped met on equal terms, members of one happy family, seeking and finding wholeness and peace.

Where words, often flagging and faltering, failed to communicate, touch with its love and affection seemed to overcome all handicap, verbal, mental and physical, and made us one.

*The hands of God have been laid
  upon our sorrowful faces,
  the hands of God have caressed our wounded hearts
  giving relief, at last, from the flames of our suffering.
  Will our hands be laid in this way too?

1

Nature of Touch

We often talk about the way we talk, and we frequently try to see the way we see, but for some reason we have rarely touched on the way we touch.

Desmond Morris, 'Intimate Behaviour' (1971)

Physical touch is one of the most basic forms of communication, and the most personally experienced of all sensations. Our deepest thoughts and fears can only be communicated by touch. Tactile sense attends awareness of ourselves and each other. Hands are the most important and tactile instruments we possess. In our technological and impersonal culture perhaps we need closeness and physical intimacy more than ever. No symbol can be as powerful as a gesture of friendship; no action as meaningful as a dimension of commitment and trust.

Paradoxically, touch can also signify violence and destruction: it can hurt and frustrate. We touch the palm of one hand with the palm of the other with fingers together as an act of prayer and devotion: we clench our fists as an act of aggression and hostility. It may be interpreted as a homosexual or sexual advance; it may be a sincere attempt to proffer help and support. Sartre saw touch as manipulation and conflict; Buber conceived of touch as an I-Thou mode. Like other methods of communication it can become habitual, banal and insincere, yet it can convey a sharing when more refined communication is hindered by anything from psychological 'defences' to impaired concentration.

'We respond to gestures', wrote Sapir (1927), 'with an extreme alertness and, one might almost say, in accordance with an elaborate and secret code that is written nowhere, known by none, and understood by all.' A warm and comfort-

3

ing touch aimed at establishing friendly relationships can offer encouragement, symbolize care and express emotional support and understanding. Being touched by another human being satisfies the need to be desired as a physical presence. One is involved and consolidated in a connected network of values with others.

Although touch is considered to be one of the most powerful of the non-verbal modalities it has received the least research attention. Its very complexity however makes it a fascinating focus for study. The functions served by various types of touch can be described as follows: *passive touch* (the act of being touched) relates to pain and communicates such information as tenderness, caring and direction. *Self-touching* can be employed for exploration, self-stimulation and self-control. *Active touching* can be used to explore, to communicate with another, to emphasize a word or a communication or to calm another. Barnett (1972) recalls that touch has been used to convey meaning since the beginning of mankind. From the earliest days touch has played a central role as an instrument of healing and as a facilitator of concern and compassion. Medical disciplines have used it extensively from the time of witch-doctors to present-day practitioners of medicine. Parents and children, lovers and friends all use touch to convey love, express empathy, and a multitude of other emotions. Touching is generally perceived as a feminine-appropriate behaviour and studies reveal that women touch and are touched more by others than men (Fisher, Rytting and Heslin, 1976). Physical contact between people plays an important role in inter-personal relations among all human cultures. The handshake, as well as various other tactile stimuli (apart from specific erogenous zones), is a well-known example of such powerful influence.

Much emphasis is placed upon verbal communication yet the non-verbal is often far more accurate in reflecting emotions and expressing true feelings. Often a verbal response proves far more significant when it is accompanied by a touch gesture. In certain circumstances words are sometimes more of a hindrance than a help. Physical touch links us to our humanness: it helps us share ourselves and our feelings with another.

Therapeutic communication during an inter-personal

encounter helps people to overcome temporary stress, get along with other people and resolve psychological blocks which stand in the path of self-realization. 'At times this process is referred to as therapy,' states Ruesch (1973) 'at other times as education; some call it counselling; others simply friendship.'

Jourard (1968) has some interesting observations on therapeutic communication through touch. He states that it is an action which bridges the gulf many people develop between themselves and others, and between their 'self' and their body. When we touch someone, we experience their body and our own simultaneously. Touching another person is the last stage in reducing distance between people. Each person lives as if with an invisible fence around his body, a fence that keeps others at that distance which he feels most safe and comfortable. We know little, he concludes, about the conditions under which a person will permit another to touch him, and little of the consequences of body contact.

We have constantly to bear in mind that each person is unique in responding to being touched and touching others. The skin serves as a demarcation zone providing a boundary between the 'me' and the 'not me'. There are those who are hurt or threatened by the breakage of a real or imagined boundary and become 'touchy'. For others there may be no breach but only harmony and empathy and they feel most 'touched'. When we misjudge the feeling of the other we risk being 'out of touch'. We develop a 'fine touch' when we instil a sense of rapport, empathy and understanding.

Touch has been described by Montagu (1971) as the 'mother of the senses', and he contends that next to the brain, the skin is the most important organ system. He schematically presents the need for touch as follows:

Physical tension	Urge of need to	Act of contact	Homeostasis
General tension	be caressed		Soothing effect

Skin is our first real medium of communication and it serves as our individual boundary and protector. It is the expression of our inner feelings; it tells us and others how we feel emotionally and it also reflects our age. The significance of the tactile functions of the skin is evident from some of the many expressions used in common parlance, and built into our very language. We refer, for example, to a deeply felt experience as 'touching'; we say that someone has 'the human touch', and we get in 'touch' or 'contact' with others. We express a desire 'to keep in touch' with certain friends and acquaintances. We use such expressions as 'rubbing someone up the wrong way'.

Montagu also reminds us that the word 'tact', derived from the Latin word meaning 'touch', was not infrequently used in England in place of the word 'touch' down to the middle of the nineteenth century. 'Tact', in its modern usage, was adopted from the French early in the same century, and what the term originally means is clearly 'to delicately touch' the other. Touch is a language which conveys meanings. It has by far the longest entry in the *Oxford English Dictionary*, occupying fourteen columns (1,500 lines) in all, which signifies the influence which tactile experience has upon our imagery and everyday speech.

Touch has universal meaning and tactile gesture forms a 'silent *lingua franca*', meaningful to all regardless of race, age, religion, mentality or socio-cultural background. As a primitive mode of communication it frequently has meaning for an individual when no other form of communication does (Critchley, 1939).

There is a wide range of attitudes and practices relating to physical touch in various cultures, and society varies from family to family and along ethnic and class lines. In some cultures it appears to be an essential part of everyday life, while in others it is discouraged. Those of Anglo-Saxon origin, the English and German in particular, are relatively non-tactual. Cultures such as Latin, Russian, Black and Jewish, are highly tactile. The French embrace and kiss their male friends – much to the embarrassment of Anglo-Saxons. Russians receive a great deal of cutaneous stimulation during their younger years, and continue their habit of tactility all through their lives. Americans are generally considered non-tactile (Montagu 1971, Frank 1957, Jourard 1966).

Different experiences within child-rearing practices may account for individual variations within these cultural groups. Elonen (1961) studied child-rearing practices in American and Finnish cultures, and found striking differences in the use of touch by parents to demonstrate affection towards their children. Affection was displayed more by means of voice fluctuations and eye glances than by fondling and kissing with Finnish infants. In Mexico and Puerto Rico many people walk arm in arm, men with men and women with women. Chinese students commonly hold hands with students of the same sex. Jourard (1966) observed pairs of people sitting in coffee shops in San Juan (Puerto Rico), London, Paris and Gainesville (Florida), counting the number of times that one person touched another at one table during a one-hour sitting. The scores were for San Juan, 180; for Paris, 110; for London, 0; and for Gainesville, 2. Anglo-Saxon Americans, Canadians and British are more reserved and distant, and seemingly uncomfortable when other people 'get too close'. In some cultures there are even laws that legislate against touching.

About one fifth of the peoples of India are the 'untouchables', the lowest of the four castes or *varna* of Hinduism – *brahmans* (priests), *kshatniyas* (soldiers), *vaisyas* (merchants) and *sudras* (untouchables). Mere contact with the 'untouchables' is contaminating. They perform the most menial of tasks. Even if their shadow falls on a person of higher caste it is thought to be defiling.

Pluckham (1968) observes how, in Western culture, a person who touches another is often quick to excuse himself. A movement of the touched person's body may convey annoyance caused by the touch or intrusion. Human beings need and use space as a protective device. Unwitting intrusions on another's 'space' may inhibit a friendly relationship; conversely, respect for it may facilitate a meaningful relationship.

As touch is rooted in antiquity so is its taboo. In past periods of history and in some cultures it would be difficult to exaggerate the importance ascribed to touch. Touch was magic, and formed an important role in primitive medicine and in tribal and religious ceremonies, and its power symbolized the gods. The outstretched hand to help and care, the laying on of hands and the comforting caress with the intent to help or heal have been very much part of all history.

How in our Western culture did the taboo on physical touch originate? Many factors seem to have contributed.

The rather mystical association of physical contact with the traditions of religion and magic may have had an influence. So too had Victorian sexual prudery. For example, Jourard and Rubin (1968) express the view that 'touching is equated with sexual intent, either consciously, or at a less-conscious level.' Lewis (1972) also suggests that 'in general, for men in our culture, proximity (touching) is restricted to the opposite sex and its function is primarily sexual in nature.' Sensuality and sexuality are all too readily confused. Touch is complicated by social norms regarding who has permission to touch whom and what is considered to be an appropriate context for touch behaviour (Heslin and Alper, 1983).

A general practitioner (Heylings, 1973) proffers some speculative questions in the attempt to diagnose 'the no touching epidemic', which is aptly described as 'an English disease'. 'How did it all develop?' he asks.

> Is our fear of sex the reason? Some people touch only during the sex act. Is Christianity to blame? Christ cured people by laying his hands on them. Is the Church at fault? High pulpits and private pews? Does the type of house we live in rub salt into the wounds of this illness? . . . could it be the fault of our parents and their parents? Yet mothers are constantly touching their babies – at least until the child starts having a will of his own. Perhaps the children antagonize their parents by a premature display of self-will. Humans stroke cats, pat dogs, snuggle up to horses without apprehension – yet they refuse this grace to human beings!

Maybe we become wary of physical touch on account of it being such a risk-filled form of human inter-personal relationships. 'I may talk to you and remain hidden from you,' writes Young (1965), 'but, if we touch, I am vulnerable, I may reveal more of myself to you than I can trust you with. There is a feeling of control in verbal discourse that is absent with physical intimacy.' We need to touch but we become fearful of the power and trust it demands. Each time we touch another we leave an impression of ourselves behind. The ritualized handshake when an introduction takes place is somewhat indicative of the ambivalence attached to physical contact with strangers.

A number of other theories have been put forward in an attempt to account for the touch taboo. Burton and Heller (1964) state that:

> Western man has shown an increasing estrangement from his body. As cultures have evolved there has been a greater tendency to relinquish sensory qualities of immediate experience for more conceptual and intellectual forms, such as language. Any deviations from this, such as touching the body, are looked upon as pathological without necessarily examining their existential meaning or genesis.

Closely akin, Jourard (1967) considers the 'touch taboo' to be part of the more general alienation process that characterizes our depersonalizing social system with its dread of authentic self-disclosure. Within such a society our bodies tend to disappear, and we lose the capacity to experience them as vital, enlivened and as the centre of our being. The restricted experience of being touched appears to be consistent with Laing's diagnosis of modern man as 'unembodied'. According to Jourard, we have come to believe that we give up the capacity to experience our body as enlivened in return for the 'benefits' of our increasingly automated and mechanized way of life. There can be loss of one's body through repression, and misuse of one's body in obsessive pursuit of security and respectability.

Mintz (1969), exploring reasons for the strong taboo regarding touch found in the psychoanalytical tradition (see p. 90), offers some historical insight. He refers to 'the desire of the early analysts to establish themselves as scientists, divorced alike from magic and from religion; and Freud's rejection of his own early use of therapeutic massage, stroking, and his experiments with the recovery of memories through hypnosis.' Because of their practices Freud and his associates were often viewed as sexual perverts. Hence it became important to avoid any physical contact with their patients, no matter how neutral its intent.

Touch establishes non-verbal communication by stimulating receptors in the skin. These transmit messages to the brain which in turn are interpreted by the individual. In the sphere of inter-personal relationships what is not said can often prove more meaningful than the spoken words. Ges-

9

tures, defined by Critchley (1939) as 'a kind of italicized speech', can effectively communicate ideas and emotions. In all human culture the touching of another is normally evidence of friendliness and affection. According to Spurgeon English, love and touch are inseparable and indivisible.

Non-verbal communication takes on prime significance in certain situations where verbal communication fails. Modalities might include: bodily movement or 'kinesic' behaviour; gestures and other bodily movements, such as facial expression, eye movement, voice qualities, touching. Words uttered are often elaborated on by a non-verbal gesture. Where verbal and non-verbal communication are incongruent a position of conflict can arise in communication (Johnson, 1965). Critchley quotes Quintilian's *Institutes of Oratory* (AD 40–99): 'If our gestures and looks are at variance with our speech; if we utter anything mournful with an air of cheerfulness or assert anything with an air of denial, not only impressiveness is wanting to our words, but even credibility.' Our gestures can give us away by contradicting what we are trying to communicate verbally. Primitive and powerful though touch can be, it can also be inexact and will be interpreted accurately or inaccurately according to other features in the context. It must be borne in mind therefore that non-verbal behaviour may on occasions serve to contradict the verbal message.

Another purpose of the non-verbal channel is that by accompanying speech it serves to reinforce more graphically what has been said although not necessarily linked with the emotional state. It also helps to emphasize parts of the verbal message. Body movements, of which physical touch may be one, can often be used to add more weight to the words or sentiments expressed (Hargie, 1987). It has been claimed by Birdwhistell (1970) that the average person actually speaks for a total of only ten to eleven minutes daily, and he estimates that in a one-to-one relationship the verbal components carry about one-third of the social meaning of the situation while the non-verbal accounts for approximately two-thirds. Non-verbal language is said to be partly taught, partly instinctive and partly imitative. The way one listens, uses silence and the sense of touch may convey important information about the private self that is not available from conversation alone.

Although we may not be aware of it, we communicate through everything we do as well as say. Thus we say 'actions speak louder than words'. The fundamental nature of trust is emphasized by Melanie Klein (1963) when she states that the need to establish non-verbal dialogue, the need to pursue understanding without words, exists in all of us.

Another non-language communication system related to touch is man's use of space, which has been defined as 'room to move about in', and 'room to put our bodies in'. In the communication process physical space symbolizes a non-verbal message between two or more people. Hall, who has studied the relationship between culture, space and communication in *The Silent Language* (1959), and *The Hidden Dimension* (1966), coined the term 'proxemics' to refer to observations of and theories about man's use of space. He identifies four distance zones commonly used by people in Western culture. These range from close, intimate distance, which includes touch, to personal and social distance, to the extreme of public distance. Our private and personal worlds are full of both real and imagined 'boundary lines' and 'territories' whose importance may be intensified when a person is in need of being recognized and respected. The positioning of one person in relation to another conveys meaning. Young children, for example, are apt to touch each other, or sit or stand close together, but as they grow older they seem to require spatial distance from others.

Morris (1982) defines the way people touch each other in public as 'a body-contact tie-sign'. When this happens he states that 'What we see is the attraction process of the bonding overcoming the natural inclination of each individual to defend his personal space. Because there is a basic conflict between "keeping your distance" and "making contact", the result is that there are many varieties and degrees of friendly touching.' He makes mention of some 457 types of body contact from which he isolates 14 major types. The basic groupings are as follows: the handshake, where a personal bond is absent, weak, or there has been a long separation; the body-guide, which often comprises a light clasp on the arm, or mild pressing of the hand on the back to direct movement; the pat, which is a type of miniature embrace performed by the hand alone. The most obvious and publicly

11

displayed is the arm-link with its symbolism of support and protection. There is the shoulder embrace and the full embrace; the latter being for intense emotional moments, although nowadays a common feature of sport. Other signs are the hand-in-hand, the waist embrace, the kiss, the hand-to-head caress, the body support, illustrated by children sitting on parents' laps or being carried when tired or during playful adolescent interludes. Finally Morris refers to 'the mock-attack' which comprises the friendly liberties taken as demonstrations of familiarity – the body-pushes, hair-rufflings, squeezes and nudges. As children we normally turned to our mothers so that when sad, stressful or in danger we might be held. As adults we often long for the tender, comforting arm on the shoulder, or pat on the hand or head.

Each of us is aware that we need space around us, and if that space is intruded upon we feel uncomfortable and threatened. Our self-identity requires that we separate ourselves conceptually from others. Psychologically we claim ownership of the space around us for personal and security reasons.

Touch is a reciprocal experience in the sense that what a person touches also touches him. 'In the very act of touching, one is touched in return. . . . In touch, the distinction between touching subject and touched object blurs' (Mazis, 1971). We do not have to look at someone who is looking at us, but it is well-nigh impossible not to touch someone who is touching us. When two people touch they eliminate the space between them. Such a gesture is a means of expressing intimacy and affection or hostility and anger. By means of physical touch we are helped to be in contact with others, and we have the capacity to use our touch to communicate with others. Often the duration, firmness and type of grip of a handshake can indicate a desire for closeness or distance.

Touch can on the one hand convey either physical or psychological intimacy, or on the other physical or psychological assault such as an invasion of the other's privacy. On the negative side communication by means of touch may make subjects feel anxious and uncomfortable. In some circumstances touch may be perceived as exploitative and/or as emphasizing the inferior status of the recipient. It has been shown, too, that the same touch may be experienced positively by one sex and negatively by the other (Fisher et al., 1976). Conceptual studies by Patterson (1976) and Fisher et al. (1976) suggest that a touch will be experienced as positive when it is seen as appropriate to the situation, does not impose a greater level of intimacy than the recipient desires, or does not communicate a negative message. Farrah (1971) outlines appropriate and inappropriate situations illustrating positive and negative usages of touch. Helpful situations include when a person is depressed or anxious and fails to respond to verbal communication; when a person needs encouragement to take a difficult step; when a person is fearful; when health workers want to show that they share another's joy or that they sympathize with another's sorrow or grief; when a person needs 'mothering'; when they 'reach out' in periods of stress or need assurance of their acceptability; when a person is disorientated, unconscious, terminally ill or dying; when they are in pain, rejected, lonely or sensorily deprived.

Among inappropriate situations Farrah includes when it is sexually suggestive, or when a person has an aversion to sex or touch; when it does not convey a 'genuine' message; when a person sees physical contact as a form of communication reserved for children or the handicapped; when a person is angry or suspicious; when the health worker feels 'unnatural' or embarrassed in touching the particular person. It is important that these various circumstances be kept in mind for touch is a most sensitive and emotive gesture.

There are four primary qualities of touch. These are described by Weiss (1986) as location, intensity, action and duration. The first of these, location, refers to the part of the individual's body that is touched. Body areas of less innervation, such as back or arm, yield dull, vaguely localized impressions: highly innervated body areas, such as face and hand, yield bright, discrete, sharply localized impressions. Intensity can be strong, moderate or weak, depending on whether the degree of skin indentation caused by the touch is deep, shallow or barely perceptible. Action is that quality of touch typified by stroking, rubbing, holding or squeezing. It is a most complex quality of touch for not only do certain actions carry socio-cultured meaning to individuals, but the different ways in which they stimulate the skin, through a combination of pressure and stretching, will convey distinctly different messages to the nervous system. Finally, duration of touch is the temporal length of the touch from initiation of inter-body contact by one individual to cessation of contact by either individual. Personal views concerning the relevance of certain tactile actions (e.g. stroking), intensity (i.e. gentleness), length or frequency may be related to the age, role and sex of the person who is doing the touching. Different types of touch may have varying psychological and social implications. The skin, being such a highly complex and versatile organ, has a wide repertoire of responses.

Our attitude towards physical contact is indicated by the fact that touching goes on all around us and is normally ignored. Most people do not often think of the use of touch in a conscious, deliberate manner, and are not aware of their own feelings about being touched unless it is brought to their attention. Tactual contact is often equated with sex unless it is perfectly clear there is no connection. It is thus used sparingly to express warmth, affection, understanding and acceptance. Perfunctory contact tends to take place between individuals of the same sex, between parents and their grown children, and in medicine, including occupational, physical and speech therapies. The touch is often mechanical and without feeling, lest too much of oneself is revealed or misinterpreted. Lovemaking apart, most of us tend to be disembodied, with our bodies disappearing from our experience (Huss, 1976).

If it is to be considered a form of communication touch must convey a message from one person to another, and if the message is to be understood communicative signals must have specific meanings to both sender and receiver. Touch accompanied by movement is the only sense that both receives and sends messages. The quality of the touch, its location, rhythm and intensity, all determine its message. Clynes (1972) describes in the following incident the use of touch to send a message. He recalls that in 1967 he took part, as pianist, in Pablo Casals' Master Classes in San Juan, Puerto Rico. One day when Casals was teaching Haydn's 'Cello Concerto', he asked a participant, a young master in his own right, to play the theme from the Third Movement. His

14

playing was expert, sure and graceful, but for Casals something was missing.

The master stopped the performance, 'No, no!' he said, waving his hands. 'That must be graceful.' He took up his own 'cello and played the same passage:

> And it was graceful, a hundred times more graceful than we had just heard. Yes – it seemed as though we had never heard grace before. We had experienced one of the least understood forms of human communication – a powerful and clear transmittal of feeling without words, a feeling that penetrated our defenses and transformed our states of mind.

Casals played the same notes and at similar speed. But the muscles of his hands and arms acted precisely together with his 'cello according to his very idea of grace.

In reminding us that with few exceptions it is the memory of tactile experiences that enables us to appreciate texture, Hall (1969) notes how a bowl that is smooth and pleasing to touch communicates not only that the artisan cared about the bowl and the person who was going to use it, but about himself as well. He describes how the rubbed-wood finishes produced by mediaeval craftsmen communicated the importance they attached to touch.

Tactile stimulation is also a powerful influence throughout the animal kingdom and this was noted by Darwin (1955), who mentions how animals have a 'strong desire to touch the beloved person . . . dogs and cats manifestly take pleasure in rubbing against their master and in being rubbed . . . monkeys delight in fondling and in being fondled.'

The earliest study of the benefits of tactile stimulation such as handling or 'gentling' on animals was on rats. Hammett (1921) observed the effects of removing the thyroid of rats in an effort to learn why many more rats in one group died. He discovered that the rats in the group with the high survival rate were routinely taken from their cages and petted by a night laboratory worker. The results of his findings were impressive: 79 per cent of the rats who were not handled died within 48 hours of the thyroidectomy operation, while only 13 per cent of the rats who were in the gentled or handled group died within the same period of time. In further studies

Hammett carried out, the gentled animals were found to be more placid while the non-gentled animals were more fearful, aggressive and excitable. Other studies on the stroking of rats have shown how touch promoted their growth (McClelland and Weininger, 1956), improved their learning processes (Levine, 1956) and affected their competitive social behaviour (Rosen, 1957).

In sport we observe automatic, almost unconscious, spontaneous physical and tactile contacts which have 'a content of giving and getting'. A rapport is initiated among the contestants. Handshakes, touches and hugs welcome a goal or a try in congratulation or acknowledgement. There is also the physical 'rough and tumble' of the game itself. Youthful adherents of various pop-groups rush forward to touch or clutch the hand of their favourite 'star' or 'idol'. At election time and during local political campaigns supporters surge towards the 'man' of their choice to shake hands, and he in turn is only too eager to reciprocate in order to gain their allegiance.

Montagu (1971) notes how touch is often used to relieve tension. In moments of anxiety or perplexity men will rub their chins with their hand, tug at the lobes of their ears and rub their forehead. They also rub the side of the neck, place flexed fingers over the mouth or pass their hands over closed eyes. Women have very different gestures such as putting a finger on their lower front teeth with the mouth slightly open or placing a finger under the chin. Other self-comforting gestures, particularly in circumstances of shock or grief, are evident in the wringing of hands and the holding on to oneself by clasping one's hands. When attempting to conceal the truth we send unconscious messages. Morris (1977) terms this 'non-verbal leakage'. There is a tendency to decrease hand gestures; hand to face contacts are increased at these moments, especially the mouth cover and the nose touch. Such gestures as these are not normally used to communicate but are used in private. In certain parts of Asia it is customary to carry on one's person a smooth-surfaced stone of amber or jade, commonly referred to as a 'finger-piece' or 'worrybead', which serves to produce a calming effect in periods of stress or indecision (c.f. the use of a rosary, where the tactile element meets a deep psychological need).

In the late sixties and early seventies 'encounter' and 'sensitivity groups' came into vogue. Members of such groups, usually adults or older adolescents, placed much emphasis on touch and touching, caressing and holding hands. In order to achieve integrated inter-personal growth and development the groups attempted 'to put people who have become dissociated back into touch with their fellow man and the world in which they are living'. Therapy was sought by means of a variety of individual and inter-personal exercises which involved physical contact and intimate relationships with other members of the group. Schutz (1967) describes some examples of the bodily contact exercises of one such encounter group:

1. To help people who are withdrawn and have difficulty in making contact with other people:
   (a) 'Blind milling'. Everyone in the room stands up and wanders round the room with their eyes shut; when they meet someone they explore each other in any way they like.
   (b) 'Break in'. Some of the group form a tight circle with inter-locking arms. The person left out tries to break through the circle in any way he can.
2. To help people who are unable to express hostility or competition:
   (a) 'The press'. Two people stand facing each other, place their hands on the other's shoulders and try to press the other to the ground.
   (b) 'Pushing'. Two people stand facing each other, clasp their hands and try and push each other backwards.
3. To help people who have difficulty in giving or receiving affection, who avoid emotional closeness:
   (a) 'Give and take affection'. One person stands in the centre of a circle with his eyes shut; the others approach him and express their feelings towards him non-verbally however they wish – usually by hugging, stroking, massaging, lifting, etc.
   (b) 'Roll and rock'. One person stands in the centre of a circle, relaxed and with his eyes shut; the group pass him round from person to person, taking his

17

> weight. The group then picks him up and sways
> him gently backwards and forwards, very quietly.

It is debatable whether such exercises have any therapeutic effect but they appear to have helped many. Others have been inclined to drop out having found the exercises too disturbing (Argyle, 1975).

In our British culture it is often considered an affront for a person of lower status to touch another of higher status (Henley, 1973). Typically, a superior-status person touches an inferior-status one (e.g. physician – patient, teacher – student, employer – employee). In an essay entitled, 'The Nature of Deference and Demeanour', Goffman (1956) wrote of the 'touch system' in a research hospital. He noted that 'the doctors touched other ranks as a means of conveying friendly support and comfort, but other ranks tended to feel that it would be presumptious for them to reciprocate a doctor's touch, let alone initiate such contact with a doctor.' Status-touch has been regarded as a non-verbal equivalent of calling another by first name: that is, used reciprocally it indicates solidarity; when non-reciprocal, it indicates status (Brown and Gilman, 1960).

In a fascinating study by Fisher et al. (1975), it was found that when men and women assistants in a university library touched the hand of a reader returning identification cards, this less than half-second contact caused the women readers not only to like the librarian but also the library better than those who were not touched.

A number of professionals touch people in the normal course of their work – doctors, nurses, dentists, health visitors, masseurs, physiotherapists, hair-dressers, beauticians. Such gestures are, however, normally carried out as a necessary function of a particular job rather than as an involvement of inter-personal relationships.

For those who are blind the idea of the world is made up of touch, sound, taste and smell. Touch in the form of the braille code has been in use since the first half of the nineteenth century, and it enables the blind to read. By running their fingers over the raised dots experienced blind people can read at the rate of fifty words per minute. When the organ of vision is put out of action the perceiving and discerning use of touch aids the blind in their recognition of materials of the physical world according to their structural qualities, and thus helps them gain experience of the world of objects.

Helen Keller, who was deaf and blind from infancy onwards, is a well-known example of how, when other senses fail, the skin is able to compensate in part for their deficiencies. The blind have to identify objects that sighted people take for granted. As one blind person remarked, 'it has to be touch, touch, touch, all the time.'

Revesz (1950) shows how tactile movements are of decisive importance for an adequate perception of spatial forms. There is touching with to and fro gliding movements used to recognize the qualities of the touched objects and variations of the surface. The sweeping touch, frequently performed with the index finger, sometimes with all three middle fingers, is efficient in the recognition of material and the examination of individual details. The transition from the sweeping touch to the grasping touch (i.e. to three-dimensional touching) is made with the assistance of the thumb. By this method two surfaces are touched simultaneously, and this enables data about structure and the arrangements of the parts of objects to become available.

Our sense of touch is the earliest to develop in the process of birth and the last to relinquish at the moment of death. In the chapters that follow an attempt is made to trace its use and significance through the various stages of human development.

Argyle, Michael	*Bodily Communication*. Methuen & Co. Ltd, London 1975.
Barnett, K.	'A survey of the current utilization of touch by health team personnel with hospitalized patients', *Int. J. Nurs. Studies*, 9 (1972), pp. 195–209.
Birdwhistell, R. L.	'Body motion', in *Natural History of an Interview*, ed. N. A. McQuown. Grung & Stratton, New York 1970.
Brown, R., and Gilman, A.	'The pronoun of power and solidarity', in *Style in Language*, ed. T. A. Sebeok. Technology Press, Cambridge 1960.

Burton, A., and Heller, L. G. — 'The touching of the body', *Psychoanal. Review*, 5 (1964), pp. 122–134.

Clynes, M. — 'Sentic cycles: the seven passions at your fingertips', *Psychology Today*, 5 (1972), p. 59.

Critchley, M. — *The Language of Gesture*. Edward Arnold & Co., London 1939.

Darwin, C. — *The Expression of the Emotions in Man and Animals*. Philosophical Library, New York 1955, pp. 213, 352.

Elonen, A. S. — 'The effect of child rearing on behavior in different cultures', *Amer. J. Orthopsychiat.*, 31 (1961), pp. 505–512.

Farrah, S. — 'The nurse – the patient – and touch', in *Current Concepts in Clinical Nursing*, eds M. Duffey, E. H. Andersen, B. S. Bergersen, M. Lohr and M. H. Rose. The C. V. Mosby Co., St Louis 1971.

Fisher, J. D., et al. — 'Hands touching hands: Affective and evaluative effects of an interpersonal touch', *Sociometry*, 39:4 (1976), pp. 416–421.

Frank, L. K. — 'Tactile Communication', *Genetic Psychology Monographs* (The Journal Press, Massachusetts) 56:2 (1957), pp. 209–255.

Goffman, E. — 'The nature of deference and demeanor', *Amer. Anthropologist*, 58 (1956), pp. 473–502. In *Interaction Ritual*, ed. E. Goffman. Anchor Books, New York 1967, pp. 47–95.

Hall, E. T. — *The Hidden Dimension*. Anchor Books, New York 1969, pp. 113–125.

Hargie, O., Saunders, C., and Dickson, D. — *Social Skills in Interpersonal Communication* (2nd edn.). Brookline Books, Massachusetts 1987.

Henley, N. M. — 'Status and sex: some touching observations', *Bull. Psychon. Soc.*, 2:2 (1973), pp. 91–93.

Heylings, P. N. K. — 'Personal view: The no touching epidemic – an English disease', *Brit. Med. J.* (14 April 1973).

Huss, A. J. — 'Touch with care or a caring touch' (1976 Eleanor Clarke Slagle Lecture), *Amer. J. Occup. Therap.*, 31:1 (1977), pp. 11–18.

Johnson, B. S.   'The meaning of touch in nursing', *Nursing Outlook*, 13 (1965), pp. 59–60.

Jourard, S. M.   *The Transparent Self.* Van Nostrad Reinhold Co. 1968.
                        'An exploratory study of body-accessibility', *Brit. J. Soc. Clin-Psychol.*, 5 (1966), pp. 221–231.

Jourard, S. M., and   'Self-disclosure and touching: a study of two
  Rubin, S. E.   modes of interpersonal encounter and their inter-relation', *J. Humanistic Psychol.*, 8 (1968), pp. 39–48.

Klein, M.   *Our Adult World and Other Essays.* Heinemann 1963.

Laing, R. D.   *The Divided Self.* Tavistock, London 1960.

Lewis, M.   'Parents and children: sex-role development', *School Review*, 80 (1972), pp. 229–240.

Levine, S.   'A further study of infantile handling and adult avoidance learning', *J. Pers.*, 25 (1956), pp. 70–80.

Mazis, G. A.   'Touch and vision: rethinking with Merleau-Ponty and Sartre on the caress', *Psychology Today*, 23 (1971), pp. 321–328.

McClelland, W. J.   'Differential handling and weight gain in the rat', *Canad. J. Psychol.*, 10 (1956), pp. 19–22.

Mintz, L. E.   'Touch and the psychoanalytic tradition', *Psychoanal. Review*, 56 (1969), pp. 365–376.

Montagu, A.   *The Human Significance of the Skin.* Columbia Univ. Press, New York 1971.

Morris, D.   *Manwatching: A Field Guide to Human Behaviour.* Jonathan Cape, London 1977.
                        The Pocket Guide to Manwatching. Triad, Panther Books 1982.
                        Intimate Behaviour. Book Club Assoc., London 1971.

Patterson, M.   'An arousal model of the inter-personal intimacy', *Psychological Review*, 83 (1976), pp. 235–245.

Pluckham, M. L.   'Space: the silent language', *Nursing Forum*, VII:4 (1968), pp. 386–397.

Revesz, G.   *Psychology and Art of the Blind.* Longmans, Green & Co. 1950.

Rosen, J.   'Dominance behavior as a function of early
                            gentling experience in the albino rat'
                            (Unpublished Master's Thesis). Univ.
                            Toronto 1957.

Ruesch, J. and   *Non Verbal Communication*. Univ. of California
  Kees. W.   Press, Berkeley and Los Angeles 1969.

Sapir, E.   'The unconscious patterning of behaviour in
                            society', in *The Unconscious: A Symposium*, ed.
                            F. S. Dummer. Knopf, New York 1927.

Weininger, O., et al.   'Gentling and weight gain in the albino rat',
                            Canad. J. Psychol., 8 (1954), pp. 147–151.

Weiss, S. J.   'Psychophysiologic effects of caregiver touch
                            on incidence of cardiac dysrhythmia', *Heart
                            and Lung*, 15:5 (1986), pp. 495–506.

Young, M. G.   'The human touch: who needs it?' in *Bridges
                            not Walls*, J. Stewart. Addison-Wesley
                            Publishing Co. Inc. 1965, pp. 98–101.

2

Touch in the Development of the Life Cycle

I was a child beneath her touch, – a man
When breast to breast we clung, even I and she, –
A spirit when her spirit looked through me.

D. G. Rossetti, 'The Kiss'

Our very first contact with the outside world and with life itself comes by means of tactile experiences. Touch ensures some contact with and perception of reality until the other senses mature. The need for human contact is innate and consistent from the time when the fetus leaves the womb and becomes physically separated from the mother. Detailed studies of new-born infants by Kravitz and Boehm (1971) revealed that within six hours of birth an infant achieves hand to mouth sucking. There is a preparatory response in which the head turns and the mouth opens in anticipation of sucking, and after repeated attempts the infant is able to get the fingers into the mouth. Fetal hand-to-mouth sucking was first observed by Liley (1965) while performing the first intrauterine fetal exchange transfusions.

One of the most fundamental and earliest attachment relationships is the bond between mother and infant. The cutaneous contact between mother and child seems to be the first language the child understands and the one he responds to the longest. The revelation of belonging and of love for the child is through touch. The great mystery of the human being is that a child is born so small, so fragile, in a state of complete helplessness. When it is born it is incapable of doing anything: its only communication is really a cry. When a small baby cries out and there is a positive response from the mother the child becomes aware that it is loved. It knows whether it is

23

loved or not by the reality of touch. It can be a distant touch as through a word, but essentially it will be the immediate touch; the touch of the mother's hands. Even a very young child will soon realize he is safe, protected, loved and seen as precious.

Frank (1957) maintains that there appears to be tactual sensitivity even in the ante-natal stage when the first sensory process becomes functional. A classic study by Hooker (1952) shows that until seven and one-half weeks gestational age the embryo shows no evidence of reflex activity. No area of the skin is sensitive to tactile stimulation. Over the next seven weeks almost the entire surface of the body becomes sensitive to touch, beginning with the lips and ending with the feet and legs. The top and back of the head remain insensitive until birth.

Throughout the gestation period the fetus receives continuous tactile stimulation from the mother's heart-beat which is transmitted and amplified through the surrounding amniotic fluid. This in turn creates a rhythmically pulsating environment. The uterine contractions are described by Montagu (1971) as 'the beginning of caressing of the baby in the right way – a caressing which should be continued in very special ways in the period immediately following birth and for a considerable time thereafter.'

Some maternity patients actively seek physical touch during this stage of uterine contraction in order to be reassured that there is someone with them at their side to enable them to maintain contact with reality. It has been found that patients are more able to work with contractions when touch is given than when touch is not given. Lesser and Keane (1956) studied a number of women in labour and found that physical contact between nurse and patient helped foster a much appreciated feeling of continuous human presence even when the nurse could not give continuous care. One woman in labour declared that she needed 'somebody that I know [to be] with me – that could either hold my hand or let me hold them.' An exploration study was undertaken by Penny (1979) using interviews with 150 postpartum women to determine their perceptions of the touch they received during labour. In response to the question, 'In general would you say that your feelings about the touch you received during labour were positive, somewhat positive, neutral, somewhat negative, or negative?' 93 women answered 'positive', 31 women answered 'somewhat positive', 14 answered 'neutral', 6 answered 'somewhat negative' and 6 answered 'negative'. A comforting reassuring touch seems therefore to have a quieting effect on the woman in labour who is facing the anxieties of the element of the unknown, the loneliness of pain, the threat to body image, dignity, privacy and self-esteem.

Recent American research indicates that mothers supported by understanding lay women companions have more comfortable births and better relationships with their babies than women who are unsupported during labour. Both mother and father often require continuous informed lay or professional support. Klaus and Kennell et al. (1986) undertook a controlled study of the effect of a supportive companion staying with women throughout labour. Continuous social support and touching of mothers during labour is a component of care in many societies but is inconsistent in our own. Social support was provided by female companions for mothers who were about to have their first babies. Compared with 249 women undergoing labour alone, 168 women, who had supportive female companions to reassure and touch them during labour, had significantly fewer perinatal complications, including caesarian sections, and fewer infants admitted to neonatal intensive care. Those with a companion also had a significantly shorter duration of labour. Social support has an impressive role in medicine (Klaus, 1988), and the study suggests that it may be of great benefit to women during labour. Touch can be an effective way to alleviate the mother's anxiety as well as to help her mobilize her resources in order to cope with her situation.

In the immediate post-natal period the new born infant is once again subjected to physical touch as he is handled, fed and bathed. Incoming sensory stimuli are mediated almost exclusively by the skin. At the mother's breast the baby hears again the rhythmic reassurance of the maternal heart-beat. The newly-born babe feels the touch of his mother before he sees her, and he senses the maternal touch as communicating security, warmth and love. Although nourishment is derived from the breast, the contact manipulation which the young infant has with the mother's breast is as important psychologi-

25

cally as the nourishment itself (Heller and Burton, 1964). In the magical moments of the first hour after birth the mother touches her child for the first time, brushing her finger-tips across his fingers and toes and putting her palms to his body in order to massage gently the soft new skin. Studies have noted that this behaviour by the mother is probably instinctive. Such contact and touching are important to the development of bonding or attachment between mother and baby. Slowly, by means of touch, the neonate learns of his mother's love. Touch is his most developed sense and touching stimulates his desire to learn and explore his world: it teaches him confidence and helps him communicate. At the beginning of the century mothers were discouraged from picking up their infants for fear of spoiling them. There was also the fear of germs and the problems of infection. Parents were advised to keep their child at arm's length. In our more enlightened era we have come to recognize that the mother-child attachment is an enduring relationship – and that it is important that mothers stroke, massage and rub the skin of the new-born.

Klaus and Kennell (1976) hold the view that temporary separation of mother and new-born infant in the post-partum period has deleterious effects on subsequent mother-child interaction. They argue that a 'sensitive period' exists immediately after birth during which 'it is necessary that the mother and father have close contact with their neonate for later development to be optimal.' Other studies have shown that skin-to-skin contact and sucking throughout the early post-partum period result in prolonged breastfeeding and more affectionate behaviour during the lying-in period. A prototype study carried out by Kennell et al. (1974) compared the maternal behaviours of two groups each of 14 mothers who were having their first child. They were randomly assigned to have different amounts of contact with their new-born infants following birth. The first group received routine hospital care, including a glimpse of the baby at birth, a brief contact for identification 6–12 hours later and reunions of 20 to 30 minutes every four hours for feeding until the mothers left the hospital. The other group received 'early and extended' contact, experiencing skin contact with their infants for one of the first two hours of life and for five extra hours on each of the three successive days of hospitalization.

At one month after birth there was no significant difference among the groups on any care-giving behaviours, but the mothers who had extended contact spent more time engaged in face-to-face fondling behaviours with their new-born infants. After one year the major difference noted was that mothers with more initial contact spent more time in soothing their infants when they cried. Later, after two years, mothers spoke to their children with fewer commands, asked more questions and used more words per sentence. At five years there was a follow-up of these children and it was found they had higher intelligence quotients and better scores on a language comprehension test.

All these studies clearly indicate that the early neonatal period is a most sensitive one for establishing bonding and for the later mother-child relationship. In addition, infants of mothers with early and extra contact appear to cry less, smile more and perform better on developmental testing. Through knowing mother by her touch and the way he is suckled and caressed the young babe communicates with mother in a reciprocal way, both mother and child evoking responses from the other.

What happens when a young baby is deprived of touch? Studies reveal that without appropriate touch and handling the infant will not thrive normally even though nourishment and other needs are thoroughly attended to. Montagu (1971) and Frank (1957) contend that because the tactual system is one of the first functional systems, the young infant uses this as a primary mode of communication. Montagu states that 'since living in a symbolic world of ideas and concepts is a most difficult and subtle achievement, denial or deprivation of primary tactile experiences may be revealed as crucial in the development of personalities and character structure, and also in the configuration of a culture.' Where there is early deprivation we note not only the physical manifestations of speech retardation, learning disabilities and other major disturbances, but also emotional and affective problems such as schizophrenia.

In the nineteenth century it was found that over half of the infants in their first year of life regularly died from a disease named 'marasmus' (a Greek term meaning 'wasting away'). The major symptom appeared to be infantile atrophy or debility. Montagu records that as late as the second decade of the twentieth century the death rate for children under one year of age in various foundling institutions throughout America was almost 100 per cent. In the post World War II years research into the cause of 'marasmus' revealed that it seemed to occur frequently among the very young in homes, hospitals and institutions amongst those who were receiving the most careful physical attention but who were deprived of mother-love. In contrast, those babies brought up in poor homes with a lack of hygenic surroundings yet with good mother care often overcame physical handicaps and flourished.

Spitz (1956) carried out a classic evaluation of the contrast between a group of children raised in a foundling home with a second group raised in a prison nursery by their own mothers. The latter group did well despite the inauspicious environment. It was revealed that although the orphanage babies were kept clean and fed adequately, they were rarely touched or handled. A large number of the young infants developed what Spitz called an 'anaclitic depression', crying easily, sleeping and eating poorly, losing weight and being unduly susceptible to infections and eczematous lesions. Withdrawal and regression to the earlier modes of functioning occurred and previously learned skills were lost. Being keenly alive to the need for contact Spitz laments that 'throughout the Western world skin contact between mother and child has been progressively and artificially reduced in an attempted denial of the importance of mother-child relations.' The research carried out by Spitz and Ribble (1943) on the development of 'marasmus' supports the theory that being touched in particular ways is rather basic to actual physical survival.

In another study by Engel and Reichsman (1956) a similar depression was observed in 'Monica', a young girl born with an oesophageal atresia which required a gastrostomy feeding stoma shortly after birth. Her mother handled and caressed the child with great reluctance for fear of damaging the opening. She was rarely ever held in anyone's arms for a period of two and a half years. Consequently 'Monica' was neglected and family conflicts were aroused, resulting in a minimum of physical stimulation. She played with her dolls but kept them

all at a distance. Suffering from a profound psychic withdrawal she was enabled to recover only after re-hospitaliz-
ation which was accompanied by a great amount of 'mothering' on the part of the staff, and the re-education of her
mother.

In the follow-up 'Monica' later bore four girls of her own.
Each of the girls she held, not in her arms, but by her knees.
When asked why she did not hold the babies in her arms she
replied: 'It's so unnatural.' Later each of the little girls
initially played with their dolls only at a distance, but when
aged 4–5 years old they began to hold them closer to them.
A comment by Winnicott is important here: 'After all she
was a baby once and she has in her the memories of being a
baby; she also has memories of being cared for, and these
memories either help or hinder her in her own experience as
a mother.' What is so crucial is that these early experiences
received of our own parenting we ourselves use to parent our
own (Klaus, 1988).

Vital as feeding is for the child, the tactile element of the
act of nursing and the tactile interplay not associated with
feeding may be just as important. The whole future learning
of the child, her speech, her cognition and symbolic recognition are all inhibited if she is deprived of tactual experience
(Frank, 1957). Anna Freud also recognized the extraordi-
narily vital role which skin contacts play in the secure, progressive unfolding of the infant's psychic development. A
strong instinctual need appears to be satisfied by the rhythmic, gentle, warm pleasure found especially among the ven-
tral surface of the body. The small infant is helped to relax
with pleasurable feelings when stroked, cuddled and massaged. 'May it be that if we massage the skin in infancy, it
may later be unnecessary for a physician to massage his
psyche?' asks Montagu (1953).

As human beings cannot be deprived of an element so vital
to their wellbeing, many scientists have worked with animals
to study what happens where there is little or no touch or
contact; or when the source of the touch is changed and when
touch is an infrequent occurrence. Some monkeys have social
traits common to those of humans and are touching and
contact animals. It has been noted how they sit so close to
each other that they touch. They handle and groom each

other and play physical contact games as they develop and grow up. In the primate the skin contacts seem to exceed food as a source of emotional gratification. As the infant monkey grows he moves about near the mother, and in her absence exploratory and play activity becomes inhibited. It has been found that when young infant monkeys are kept separated from their mothers at birth and reared in isolation they do not grow and develop normally. When they are deprived of maternal touching they become emotionally and physically isolated and hug and rock themselves and suck their thumbs. When introduced into a group of other play-mates at five or six months of age they have no sense of play or recreation. These very same monkeys when returned to their mothers after only six weeks of separation develop into normal young monkeys again. We can only learn to love by first being loved ourselves (cf. 'We love because he first loved us', 1 John 4:19).

The classic studies of Harlow (1958) have shown the significance of physical contact between the monkey mother and her infant for the subsequent healthy development of the latter. To carry out his experiments he decided to erect a terry-cloth surrogate mother with a light bulb behind her which radiated heat and warmth. Such a 'mother' was 'soft, warm and tender, a mother with infinite patience, a mother available twenty-four hours a day, a mother that never scolded her infant and never struck or hit her baby in anger.' Another surrogate mother was built entirely of wire mesh without the terry-cloth 'skin', and was thus lacking in contact comfort. Harlow reports: '. . . the dual-mother surrogate condition, a cloth mother and a wire mother, were placed in different cubicles attached to the infants' living cage . . . for four new-born monkeys the cloth mother lactated and the wire mother did not; and for the other four, this condition was reversed.' In every case quoted the infant preferred the cloth toy to the wire feeder and returned to it for comfort, contact and solace. 'Certainly, man cannot live by milk alone', concludes Harlow. 'Love is an emotion that does not need to be bottle or spoon-fed, and we may be sure that there is nothing to be gained by giving lip-service to love.'

From the time they are born young babies need to be touched, held and caressed. Play forms an important part in their development. Touch through play is a communication of love. The child senses the laughter, the joyfulness in the mother. In play mother and child revel in the full indulgence of their sense of touch with all the strength of emotion it can arouse. It is through body contact that they are enfolded in a new dimension of experience; the experience of the world of the other. It is this bodily contact with the other that provides the essential sources of comfort, security, warmth and increasing aptitude for new experiences. Winnicott (1965) and Bowlby (1969) studied the contributions of dynamic psychology on these early formative years of mother-child relationship, and both stress the important contribution of physical touch. There is in infants an in-built need to be in touch with and to cling to a human being. Bowlby (1969) concentrated on the human capacity to form bonds of attachment, and considered that important as food is to the small infant, it does not compare in significance with the instinctive bonds of attachment which depend on sight, sound and touch. This attachment establishes a powerful bond between mother and child through which the infant feels recognized, wanted, appreciated – in other words, loved. The mother's capacity to identify with her baby allows her to fulfil the function described by Winnicott (1965) as 'holding' – 'the basis for what gradually becomes a self-experiencing being.' He describes the function of holding as a protection from physiological insult. It takes account of the infant's skin sensitivity – touch, temperament, auditory sensitivity, visual sensitivity – and of the infant's lack of knowledge of the existence of anything other than the self. It also follows the minute day-to-day changes belonging to the infant's growth and development, both physical and psychological.

Babies seem to differ in their acceptance of and response to tactile approaches. Mothers, too, vary in their attitudes. There are many who very generously provide opportunities of touch while some deny or deprive their young of such tactile ministrations. In these circumstances a baby will often become attached to a substitute contact, a 'surrogate', such as a cuddly toy, blanket, thumb-sucking or fingering of hair. The child's whole perception of the environment is developed through tactile experiences. The manner in which she is washed and bathed, put to bed and clothed, all influence her subsequent learning capabilities and individual patterns of communication with others. As the baby grows and develops stability (*homeostasis*) she becomes less and less dependent upon touch. She develops linguistic communication to orientate herself.

Some psychologists believe the new-born infant to be traumatized by birth. After nine months in a warm, dark and cushioned environment the newly born babe has suddenly to adjust to a cool, brightly lit and often noisy world. Leboyer (1975), in his *Birth Without Violence*, advocates that the separation of the newly born from the prenatal environment be as gradual as possible. He demonstrates how he places the infant on the mother's abdomen immediately after birth. He covers the body of the babe with the hands, strokes it gently and encourages the mother to keep the baby as close to her as possible. He suggests that the baby be left attached to the mother through the umbilical cord until respiration is established. Throughout this period the baby lies on the mother's abdomen partially covered by the hand of the midwife or attendant physician. Leboyer advocates that this soothing treatment of the new-born is probably the most important step in developing healthy human relations.

> Being touched and caressed,
> being massaged,
> is food for the infant.
> Food as necessary
> as minerals, vitamins, and proteins.
> Deprived of this food,
> the name of which is love,
> babies would rather die.
> And they often do.
>
> (Leboyer, 1977)

A definite progression and orderly sequence in the nature and amount of contact a mother makes with her baby has been noted by Rubin (1963). She observed how from small areas of physical contact the mother gradually moves to more extensive ones. At first she uses only her finger-tips, then her hands including the palms and finally much later her arms as an extension of her whole body. In this way the mother is alert for positive signs of mutuality in order that a progressive

32

relationship might be established. Sometime within the period of 3–5 days the mother will often advance from the touch of her finger-tips to the whole cupped hand to stroke the baby's head. Rubin also makes the interesting comment that:

> mothers who have had a very recent experience and meaningful bodily touch from a ministering person, as during labour, delivery or the postpartum period, use their own hands more effectively. This is true of both . . . first-time mothers and . . . mothers who have had more than one child. Conversely, if the mother's most recent experiences of contact in relation to her own body have been of a remote and impersonal nature, she seems to stay longer at this stage in her own activities with the baby.

Such observations give strong credence to the practice of regular physical caressing by the husband of his wife during the stages of pregnancy, labour and immediately after birth of the baby.

The human emotional need for physical contact has been established through prospective and retrospective psychoanalytic studies (see p. 94) and theorists state that the early life of the infant is crucial to his later emotional well-being (A. Freud, 1952: Erikson, 1963). It has been maintained by Schilder (1950) that 'the touches of others, the interest others take in the different parts of our body, will be of enormous importance in the development of the postural model (i.e. body image) of the body.' His findings have been interpreted by other researchers as further support for their thesis regarding the importance of maternal care to the development of the child's body images, and in turn to the formation of the child's sense of self. Early maternal touch is essential for the process of maternal-infant attachment to occur (Klaus and Kennell, 1970: Winnicott, 1970: Montagu, 1978).

A study designed by Anisfeld and Lipper (1983) explored further the hypothesis that a period of close contact between mother and infant immediately after birth facilitates the establishment of a close bond. Fifty-nine women between the ages of 17 and 38 years who had given birth were admitted to the study. Two sets of equally acceptable postpartum procedures were worked out with the delivery room staff. One procedure was termed 'extra contact' (E.C.), and the other 'routine care' (R.C.). In the E.C. procedure, immediately after birth the baby was placed skin-to-skin on the mother's abdomen. The baby remained on the mother's abdomen during the entire stay in the recovery room for a total period of 45 to 60 minutes from the time of birth. The baby was then transferred to the nursery.

In the R.C. procedure, the baby was taken to an infant warmer immediately after delivery, wrapped in a sheet, briefly shown to the mother and then transferred to the nursery within 15 to 20 minutes of birth. Observations of maternal behaviour during feeding were made two days after birth by an observer blind to the randomization status of the mother. The mothers who received 'extra contact' exhibited significantly more affectionate behaviour toward their infants than did the mothers who received 'routine care'. In this study, the only difference in treatment between the E.C. and R.C. groups was the 45–60 minutes period of extra contact immediately after birth. The findings would therefore suggest that even as little as one hour of extra contact can influence the amount of affectionate behaviour a mother shows toward her infant.

Using filmed observations Klaus, Kennell, et al. (1970) revealed how the human mother, as in other animal species, demonstrates an orderly progression of behaviour after she gives birth. When nude full-term infants were brought to their mothers shortly after birth the mothers commenced a routine pattern of behaviour which began with fingertip touching of the infant's extremities and proceeded in 4 to 8 minutes to massaging and encompassing palm contact on the trunk. In the first 3 minutes, the extent of fingertip contact was 52 per cent, 28 per cent being palm contact. In the last three minutes of observation, fingertip contact had markedly decreased. As previously noted, Rubin (1963) observed a similar sequence but at a much slower rate (3 days).

Psychologists have observed that babies who are handled the most cry less and make fewer demands by the time they are one year old. Handled babies feel reassured and secure, and because they are less afraid have less to cry about. Further research is confirming the importance of human touch in the parent-child relationship.

One of the most basic needs to be met and reinforced in a

child, according to Erikson (1959), is the ability of an infant to develop trust; the modalities being the need 'to get' and 'to give in return'. Rubin (1963) demonstrates that implicitly underlying the various studies on touch is the high adaptive value of the tactile sense when other sensory apparatuses are inadequate.

In our own culture at a certain stage we cease touching children: we teach them to keep their hands to themselves, not even to explore themselves. Children who touch their bodies are often punished, and are told to keep their bodies at a distance. If they touch other things they are warned: 'Don't touch', and such an order soon becomes a childhood litany. They absorb from the adult world the concept that touching the human body is indecent. Anderson (1979) undertook a project with 803 elementary schoolchildren to define different types of touch. From the children themselves a number of important factors come to light. One was that children can tell the difference between touch which they experience to be caring and touch which is exploitative.

As the child grows up touching with parents is not as frequent and not as intimate. Gradually a detachment period begins. Many studies quoted have observed the importance of attachment between mothers and children, but little seems to have been written about the importance of detachment between parents and children. Throughout the teenage years there is a growing intimacy and touch with one's peers. A study by Jourard (1965) noted that few students were touched anywhere by their parents beyond the hands and arms. Anderson (1979) recognizes that although we now know more about the damage of no touch in early infancy, we still know very little about specific touching needs throughout life.

Throughout childhood physical touch becomes a means of learning and discovering. This is the period of major development of two perceptual systems which Balint (1968) describes as 'sight-orientated' and 'touch-orientated'. He sees the latter as both more immediate and more friendly than the former, in which space is friendly but is filled with dangerous and unpredictable objects (i.e. people)!

Unfortunately the only physical intimacy some children are able to get is when they misbehave, for sadly the need to touch can also be expressed in acts of hostility. This is evidenced in

35

much child-abuse, which may be viewed as a disorder of touch. The battered child syndrome also provides the most dramatic evidence of a disorder of mothering. Multiple factors contribute to the problem, for abusing parents have wide-ranging, diffuse and interrelated problems, but early separation may prove to be a significant one (see p. 96). The formation of close affectional ties may remain permanently incomplete if extended separation occurs and anticipatory grief becomes too far advanced (Klaus and Kennell, 1970).

Many studies reveal that a prolonged period of maternal deprivation, where there has been a loss of rewarding tactual stimulation, may have a lasting detrimental effect on the eventual character and life-style of the infant. For example, one study (Greenwald, 1958) of 'call girls' observed that the girls discovered at an early age that their feelings of isolation and loneliness, and their needs for affection, could be satisfied through sexual gratification. Such physical contact compensated for the closeness denied them by their parents.

As learning develops sensory touching is replaced by visual touching. Parents touch their offspring more between the ages of one to two, when they are first walking, but touch appears to decline after this preliminary stage. Girls appear to be touched more frequently than boys. Between the ages of 5 to 16 years, although the need for tactual contacts seem to diminish, the desire to touch and to be touched seems to increase suddenly at puberty, first between members of the same sex and then heterosexually. Up to the ages of 10 to 12 years young children continue to touch their parents and in the course of a variety of games, friendly squabbles and fighting, they also touch other children of the same sex a great deal. 'Touching parents expresses a close and dependent attitude, while touching other children is affiliative or aggressive' (Mitchell 1975). As the years progress in adolescence there is much need for closeness and intimacy, and for physical contact. At this stage touching can be associated and equated with sex.

Throughout adult life physical contact appears to be severely restricted. Argyle (1975) lists a number of socially defined circumstances where such contact is acknowledged as permissible: (a) with one's spouse, both during sexual activity and in the more casual circumstances of everyday domestic life; (b) with children, up to adolescence; (c) with other relations and friends in various kinds of greetings and farewells, including handshakes and embraces; and (d) between relative strangers, and in public places, bodily contact is rare. A variety of sports involve physical touching as do certain ceremonies and rituals such as baptism, marriage and graduation. As the years go by touching patterns change, and each age has distinct needs relating to giving and receiving of touch.

Anderson, D.	'Touching: When is it caring and nurturing or when is it exploitative and damaging?', *Child Abuse and Neglect*, 3 (1979), pp. 793–794.
Ainsfield, E., and Lipper, E.	'Early contact, social support, and mother-infant bonding', *Pediatrics*, 72:1 (1983), pp. 79–83.
Argyle, M.	*Bodily Communication*. Methuen & Co. Ltd., London 1975.
Balint, M.	*The Basic Fault*. Tavistock Publ., London 1963.
Bowlby, J.	'Attachment', *International Psychoanalytical Library*, (Vol. 1). Hogarth Press, London 1969.
Burton, A., and Heller, L. G.	'The touching of the body', *Psychoanal. Review*, 51 (1964), pp. 122–134.
Engel, G. L., and Reichsman, F., et al.	'A study of an infant with a gastric fistula', *Psychosom. Med.*, 18 (1956), pp. 374–384.
Erikson, E. H.	'Identity and the life cycle: selected papers', *Psychol. Issues*, 1 (1959), pp. 1–171.
Frank, L. K.	'Tactile communication: genetic psychology monographs', *The Journal Press*, 56:2 (1957), pp. 209–255.
Freud, A.	'The role of bodily illness in the mental life of the child', *The Psychoanal. Study of the Child*, 7 (1952), pp. 69–81.
Fromm-Reichmann, F.	*Principles of Intensive Psychotherapy*. Univ. Chicago Press, Chicago 1950.

Greenwald, H.   *The Call Girl*. Ballantine Books, New York 1958.

Harlow, H. F.   'The nature of love', *The American Psychologist*, 13:6 (1958), pp. 673–685.

Hooker, D.   *The Prenatal Origins of Behavior*. Univ. of Kansas Press, New York 1971.

Jourard, S. M.   'An exploratory study of body-accessibility', *Brit. J. Social and Clinical Psychiatry*, 15 (1963), pp. 221–231.

Kennell, J. H.   'Maternal behavior one year after early and extended post-partum contact', *Dev. Med. Child. Neurol.*, 16 (1974), pp. 172–179.

Klaus, M. H., and Kennell, J. H., et al.   'Mothers Separated from their New-born Infants', *Ped. Clinics N. Amer.*, 17:4 (1970), pp. 1015–1022.
Maternal-Infant Bonding. Mosby, St. Louis 1976.
'Effects of social support during parturition on maternal and infant morbidity', *Brit. Med. J.*, 293 (1986), pp. 585–587.

Klaus, M. H.   Personal communication (1988).

Kravitz, H., and Boeam   'Rhythmic habit patterns in infancy: their sequence, age of onset and frequency', *Child Development*, 42 (1971), pp. 399–413.

Leboyer, F.   *Birth Without Violence*. Alfred A. Knopf, New York 1975.
Loving Hands. Collins, London 1977.

Lesser, M. S., and Keane, V. R.   *Nurse-Patient Relationships in a Hospital Maternity Service*. C. V. Mosby Co., St Louis 1956.

Liley, A. W.   *Studies in Physiology*. Springer, Berlin 1965.

Montagu, A.   *The Human Significance of the Skin*. Columbia University Press, New York 1971.
'The sensory influences of the skin', *Texas Reports on Biol. and Med.*, 11 (1953), pp. 291–301.

Penny, K, S.   'Postpartum perceptions of touch received during labor', *Research in Nursing and Health*, 2:1 (1979), pp. 9–16.

Rubin, R.   Maternal touch', *Nursing Outlook*, Part II (Nov. 1963), pp. 828–831.

Schilder, P.   *The Image and Appearance of the Human Body*. International Universities Press 1950.

| Spitz, R. | In *Mental Health and Infant Development*, ed. K. Soddy. Basic Books Inc. Publ. New York 1956. |
| Winnicott, D. W. | *The Family and Individual Development*. Tavistock Publ., London 1965. 'The maturational processes and the facilitating environment', *Inter. Psychoanalytical Library*. Hogarth Press, London 1965. |

3

Touch in the Care of the Sick

I believe that most of us, when we are sick, need physical contact and the spoken assurance of God's love.

Michael Mayne, 'A Year Lost and Found' (1987)

The experience of illness is a complex psychological situation. Anxiety, depression, denial and regression are some of the common psychological responses. In sickness and in hospital care a patient experiences the anxiety of disintegration. Needs for safety and security undoubtedly increase and physical contact becomes of great importance. In such emotional regression every opportunity is taken to hold on to a hand or arm with the same tenacious clinging of a frightened child. It is just as important for physicians, carers and nurses to learn to use their hands in this way as to perform the most delicate medical, surgical or nursing procedures (Dominian, 1971). The increasing sophistication in medical and surgical technology in dealing with previously fatal illnesses, and the patient's relationship and dependence upon machines, also give rise to the importance of human relationships and the awareness of some of the psychological conflicts with which both staff and patient may have to wrestle. The highly scientific nature of medical diagnosis, the physical paraphernalia of many diagnostic processes, the technical language of medicine, all arouse anxiety because of fantasized dangers and unfamiliarity with what one may expect.

Holding someone's hand in conditions of stress and anxiety gives a sick person a feeling of greater security. The famous aphorism of Osler, 'Taking a lady's hand gives her confidence in her physician', illustrates the point. When illness becomes a traumatic event in one's life the individual experiences

40

anxiety, insecurity and low self-esteem. The more serious and prolonged the illness, the greater are the opportunities for anxiety to threaten the patient.

In discussing the state of anxiety Rollo May (1940) described it as a 'diffuse apprehension'. Its special characteristics are feelings of uncertainty and helplessness in the face of danger. As sick people face new threats to their very existence as persons, feelings of vulnerability, helplessness and anger are common. Anxiety arises from a realistic appraisal of danger. Admission to hospital and removal from the familiar family and social environment creates in the majority of patients a certain amount of stress and uncertainty. When a person becomes ill he is expected temporarily to give up the responsibilities of a mature adult and place his life both symbolically and realistically into the hands of another.

Duff and Hollingshead (1968) in their study, *Sickness and Society*, which deals with a most comprehensive description of the entire social structure of the general hospital and the inter-personal relationships between patients, nurses, physicians and administrators, conclude:

> When a patient enters the hospital he enters not only with his physical ailment but also with a great deal of anxiety and fear regarding his illness. Whether expressed or not, the fear of suffering, invalidism and death is always present. Many hospital situations mobilize this anxiety, among them ward rounds. Ward rounds represent an acute stressful situation to the patient because at this time he believes he is undergoing an examination that will decide his fate. The doctors represent in the patient's fantasies godlike figures who will pass judgement on him.

Adults appear to have a great need for an acceptance of affective touching during illness because of an increased need for security, rest and comfort (Bowlby, 1958: Dominian, 1971). Hospitalization has been described as an 'experience in distancing' (Ardrey, 1966).

A medical director records how, when he became a patient, he entered into a whole new world of instability and anxiety:

> I think it important to state that being a patient is an intensely personal experience that we all approach for dif-

fering reasons and with different expectations. Because of this, one thing I have learnt is that no one can truly say, 'I know how you feel' . . . life as a patient is totally different from what you expected . . . and what you would like it to be. Day merges into night and nights seem to go on for ever. Time has no relevance . . . even if you have your own room, there never seems to be enough easily accessible space. (Marsh, 1987)

The sick individual is placed in a world apart. He is in a strange environment among unfamiliar artefacts, attire and terminology: he is isolated from the healthy, as well as family and friends. He is expected to conform to institutional scheduling. The world seems to be reduced to the confines of the sick-room, and waiting involves much solitude and often lowered self-esteem. He is afraid of the loneliness, the weakness, the suffering and pain which may await him. He is alone, cut off from his former way of life, feels uncertain of the future and loses confidence in the integrity of his body which seems to have so cruelly and often suddenly betrayed him (Ardrey, 1966).

Under such circumstances no other means of communication compares with the comforting reassuring effects of physical touch. Lucente and Fleck (1972) found that a patient's level of anxiety was determined to a great extent by his personality and view of the hospital environment, rather than the severity of his condition or diagnosis. Anxiety is a sense of threat to one's wellbeing, either physically or psychologically. Often deep and personal emotional feelings and fears can be truly shared only by the touch of another. The eloquence of touch can cause the release and outpouring of pent-up emotions and is one of the most powerful means of communication (Young, 1977). Being touched is a very vital part of our interaction with others and involves a communication of love and security, which has implications for physical survival as well as emotional self-esteem.

Goffman (1967), a sociologist, refers to the 'stripping process' which characterizes the point of entry to some institutions. This, he suggests, can also imply the stripping of identity and responsibility. The arm-band or tag, for example, given to the patient for hospital identity cannot only symbolize, 'now you are tagged', but also 'now whatever happens to you is our responsibility and not yours'.

Illness can so easily lead one into a social setting which is similar to that of childhood and this is conducive to traits of behaviour used earlier in infancy. Actions, thoughts, feelings are regressive in response to the child-like world of illness. Since others seem to have assumed all responsibility for the patient's life and activity, he is now free to react as he did when he was a child. Frightened and anxious for his physical health and the revelation of his true self he has no choice but to escape into a more pleasurable period which is his past. Consequently sickness behaviour can often lead to egocentricity and emotional dependency. 'How sickness enlarges the dimensions of a man's self to himself', wrote Charles Lamb in his essay entitled 'The Convalescent'. 'He is his own exclusive object. Supreme selfishness is inculcated upon him as his only duty.' The patient who is worried or fearful will derive much comfort and self-assurance from holding a hand, or from a securing touch. Physical contact plays a large part in a helping and supportive relationship.

Understanding and appreciation of spatial factors are vital in the effective care of sick people. Heyter (1981) defines personal territory as a situation which provides security, privacy, autonomy and self-identity, all of which are important for well-being. In sickness a person's security is apt to be threatened. He becomes less tolerant of invasion of his territory and yet, in a paradoxical way, less able to defend it. He has to stay in bed and allow a host of strangers to observe, move and monitor his body and disease. Man's instinctive territoriality represents his basic need for identity. 'If territorial instincts are operant, then the patient is the transgressor into the nurses' territory and already feels a burden of guilt and tension. Far from the centre of his own ecologic domain, he is timid and apologetic, and more likely to lose any battles on this unfamiliar ground' (Minckley, 1968). The positioning of a helper or comforter in relation to one who is confined to a sickroom conveys much meaning.

Minckley, recognizing that a need for place and space is instinctive in man, studied the reaction of patients as they regained consciousness following surgery. She observed many patients as they came into and left a 10-bed recovery room over a period of several months with the purpose of looking for signs and symbolic gestures that might have territorial meaning. The initial, most common, observation was that as they began to awaken, patients generally touched the side rails of their theatre trolley first, either grasping or sliding their fingers along the rails. It appeared that in most cases, following general anaesthesia, the first orientation to environment and re-establishment of identity was tactile. The specific action of feeling or grasping the rails seemed to set in motion the process of memory recall: it was the beginning of an answer to the unspoken question, 'Where am I?' Hall's (1966) observation is relevant here: '. . . the realization of the self as we know it is intimately associated with the process of making boundaries explicit.'

To meet the total needs of sick people professional carers, be they doctors, nurses, social workers or hospital chaplains, should promote a climate conducive for patients to reveal their true selves. Physical touch has the potential for being one of the most meaningful modes of communication to encourage such a free inter-play.

It is important nevertheless for the care-giver to be aware that patients react quite differently to being touched. The effects of touch may either be positive or negative. A study by Walker (1971) showed that communication by means of touch made some people feel anxious and uncomfortable, and Henley (1973) suggested that touch may be seen as exploitative and as highlighting the lower status of the recipient. Research on sex differences reveals that males are generally more uncomfortable with dependency than females. Female patients may interpret touch as a primarily positive message of caring and warmth, while male patients may react negatively because they interpret touch as conveying a message of relative inferiority and dependency. Other studies reveal that the patients most frequently touched are those aged between 26 and 33, and those touched least are pre-adolescents and those over 66 years (Barnett, 1972: Goodykoontz, 1979).

Touching is an important part of ministering to the sick, not only as a vital aid to assessment, but also as a valuable form of communication. When it is perceived as a caring, supportive gesture, touch can help break down communication barriers which may exist. The way sick people tolerate and interpret touch varies with their previous experience, cultural background and social maturity. As a physical gesture touch therefore must be used with the utmost discretion and sensitivity. Verbal and non-verbal behaviour have to be in complete harmony otherwise sincerity will be questioned. An irritating tone of voice coupled by a gesture of touch intended to convey love, support and comfort will prove meaningless. As each person's attitude towards touching will have to be keenly observed so too will the care-givers have to be aware of their own personal feelings about it. Both carer and cared for have to be comfortable with touch (see p. 10).

The majority of sick people feel assured when someone is willing to listen to them and to value them as persons, accepting what they say without condemning them for expressing what they feel. They are helped, too, when they feel that those who minister to them have a respect for them, understand them, and assist them with recognizing and developing their resources and thereby restoring their confidence in themselves. Physical touch alone cannot eliminate a patient's anxiety completely or ensure his being relaxed, yet it can help him cope with his fears and to co-operate. As a method of caring and establishing rapport, touch can convey interest rather than indifference, approval rather than disapproval, and self-confidence rather than anxiety.

To a patient in periods of isolation and loneliness the touch of another can help break down feelings of being unloved or rejected. 'Loneliness is a world apart from others – a frightening world.' The use of touch as a communicative means can help the lonely person re-establish inter-personal intimacy and decrease the pain of isolation. On the other hand, to force touch on a lonely patient before he is ready for it will have detrimental effects. Not every person, as we have seen, is comfortable with touch. Burnside (1981) has pointed out how non-affectionate persons may be threatened by affectionate persons.

Of all the medical disciplines and healing professions nursing is one of the few which carries out a major portion of its functions through touching patients (Johnson, 1965). It seems that a generation or so ago nurses were more inclined to communicate with their patients through touch than they are today. A physician describing his experience as a hospital patient wrote: 'By entering the hospital as a patient I was exposing myself to all the indignities, to the loss of privacy that are part of the nature of institutions in general and hospitals in particular' (Abram, 1969). The greater the patient's feelings of depersonalization the greater his need for identity through physical contact.

Mead (1956) observes that the term 'compassionate' has always evoked an image of someone who lays her hands gently on the suffering, the frightened, the grief-stricken. She considers that nursing is the place, more than any other, where we can reconstitute people's faith in the relationship between their hands and their hearts and their heads: this is one of the few places where it is possible to experience the importance of human hands. 'The one place where all of us have an opportunity to really experience compassion in its complete, disciplined sensitive form is in the compassion of a nurse's hands, laid on the suffering child or closing the eyelids of the dead.' Watson (1975) divided touch into two distinct categories: *instrumental* touch which is a deliberate physical contact needed to perform a specific task (a nurse dressing a post-operative incision), and *expressive* touch which is a relatively spontaneous and affective contact which is not necessarily an essential component of a physical task (a nurse holding a patient's hand to comfort or reassure). Nursing research appears to have focussed primarily on task-related touch to the neglect of supportive comforting touch. 'During my hospitalizations,' writes Huss (1977),

> I became very sensitive to the difference between perfunctory touch and a caring touch, and their effect on my *homeostasis* (wellbeing). During a one-month stay two years ago, I was the recipient of physical and occupational therapy as well as of the care of many nurses and physicians. I became aware of the fact that most communication was carried on in the 4 – 12 foot social distance range. When it was necessary to be close, the nonverbal message was still, for the most part, that of the greater distance. When touch was necessary, it was mechanical and gave no message of caring. Instead, it was a job to be performed . . . I became acutely aware of the effects of sensory-tactile-

deprivation ... I was experiencing what Dominian calls the 'anxiety of disintegration', since my body refused to perform its daily tasks. At such times, physical contact is of great importance.

Burnside maintains that all too frequently nurses view touch as related only to tasks to be carried out as part of nursing procedures, thus conveying the message: 'I have to touch you.' If, however, a nurse touches a patient when no procedural task is involved, she is clearly saying, 'I don't have to touch you, but I want to.' She contends that such touching is a powerful therapeutic intervention, for a patient can so easily begin to feel that she is being perceived only in terms of a 'task' to be performed rather than a human being to be nursed. Basic as it may seem to hold a hand, to pat a shoulder, such a gesture can readily convey a message that indicates she is a loveable and touchable person.

A study carried out by McCorkle (1974) on the effect of touch or non-touch on 60 seriously ill patients in a general hospital demonstrated that the nurse can establish rapport with a seriously ill patient in a relatively short time through the use of touch. Out of the 30 patients touched by the nurse as part of the experimental group, 28 responded positively to the nurse-patient reaction; 21 out of the control group, who were not touched, responded positively. The analysis of the data showed that although patients may not be aware of the nurses' touch, they may be more aware of the nurses' concern, caring and interest when physical touch is employed. Langland and Panicucci (1982) also found that a significant increase in patient communication-response occurred when physical touch was used. They suggest that nurse-patient touch represents an important and effective communication tool. The core of touch lies in its unique way of communicating without words, and it becomes one of the primary ways for the professional carer to establish empathy, thereby signifying, 'I am with you and I am prepared to stay.' It is extremely important for those who tend the sick to understand that when and how they touch a patient will, in all probability, effect whatever verbal structure they themselves have set up within the relationship with a patient (Johnson, 1965).

Touch is often found effective during periods of pain.

Because pain and anxiety are often closely connected, tactile contact may help relax the patient enough to break the pain cycle. A hospice worker writes: 'We find that pain is more difficult to control in those who are very anxious and afraid . . . in the day hospice, patients whose symptoms have not responded well to treatment are absorbed by the companion-ship and relaxed atmosphere, and their conditions seem to improve.'

Under stressful situations a patient may reach out to take another's hand when a firm touch seems effective. In less acute anxiety states a tender stroking hand may be helpful. The holding of a patient's hand may reduce anxiety and meet the dependency needs that may result from pain. A study carried out by Durr (1971) suggested that physical contact and closeness can be therapeutic. Some persons may see physical contact and closeness as the only way of meeting their needs within a variety of situations. Mercer (1966) sug-gested that those who are skilled in the art of non-verbal communication should be able to use touch in a most natural way when caring for their patients.

In stressing the importance of nurses being trained to listen to patients, establish empathy and exercise touch, one member of the nursing profession writes in words which are of prime importance to all who minister to the needs of sick people:

> A touch that shows we feel close to the patient: a touch to show we understand the loneliness: a touch to show we understand pain: a touch to show we understand fear: a touch to show we understand the 'today' the patient is forced to cope with: a touch to show we are here and ready to help the patient: that touch is an indispensable ingredient in nursing, something a nurse can offer a patient that no other person has the opportunity to do on a day-to-day continuing basis. (Meredith, 1978)

In a study concerning medical-surgical nurses and the use of touch in patient situations not involving direct physical care, undertaken by Farrah (1969), 49 registered medical-surgical nurses were interviewed. The use of touch was found to be used to a far greater extent than initially predicted. The research revealed several themes that added depth and clarification to the study findings. The gesture of touch was generally seen as communicating a feeling of 'I care', of establishing and maintaining openness of communication and development of rapport and of transcending oral communication in some patient-care situations. It was also noted how touch promotes contact with reality, with the recommendation that it should be used more in nurse-patient relationships. 'Touch in conjunction with verbal responses' and 'verbal responses alone' were ranked as more preferable than 'touch alone'.

Nurses in the study also reported the following limitations of touch in its use with their patients – touch may easily be misconstrued; social mores and taboo; individual nurse's comfort as the initiator of touch, and individual patient's comfort as the recipient of touch. Over one third of the total sample of nurses felt that the individual character of the nurse was important. They stated that the nurse should not use touch unless she felt natural, comfortable or genuine in doing so. A number of nurses specifically responded that their use of touch depended on the individual patient, length and stage of the nurse-patient relationship, and the patient's feelings concerning touch and being touched.

Subjective responses to a questionnaire on the use of touch (Farrah, 1971) revealed how age, sex and medical circumstances seem to influence the nurse's approach. Nurses appeared to be more ready to touch older than younger patients, regardless of sex, and were more likely to touch female than male patients. It was reported that physical contact was used more frequently with the elderly because 'touch helps bridge the communication gap', and 'the elderly seem to appreciate this form of non-verbal support and respond to touch – they actually initiate the use of touch by reaching out for the nurse's hand.' Physical touch with a male patient was seen by some nurses as being too personal or in some way detracting from the male patient's masculinity.

In a study undertaken by the author some of the factors which effected the nurses' use of touch with their patients were described as follows: 'when a patient has received bad news or is emotionally upset' (Ward Sister): 'to reassure a patient; when talking cannot help a situation perhaps just holding their hand is all they require and often proves more beneficial' (psychiatric pupil nurse): 'when I cannot find suitable words to comfort or console a patient' (2nd year student nurse). In outlining the effect of touch on the moods, emotions and wellbeing of their patients nurses reported: 'usually they appear more relaxed and seem to be reassured by physical presence' (Staff Nurse); 'touch brings people together, helps them express their problems and emotions more freely' (2nd year student nurse); 'they feel accepted, as if they've got someone who will understand them; who is on their side. They feel as if the barriers are coming down that uniforms and status are apt to impose' (2nd year student nurse); 'those who accept touch I feel are comforted and reassured. Hopefully their mood is lifted and a sense of wellbeing enhanced. Those who do not accept touch perhaps find it embarrassing and feel uncomfortable in that situation' (3rd year student nurse); 'touch gives the patient something to "hold on to", helping them therefore to feel more secure' (2nd year student nurse): 'enables them to open up and talk to you' (2nd year student nurse): 'it makes most patients feel that somebody cares and wants to listen to what they have to say' (3rd year student). All of this confirms that the individual needs of the patient should determine the use of touch rather than the predetermined bias of the nurse.

There appears to be a present-day emphasis on ever-increasing competency and involvement in the technical skills of nursing procedures, with a corresponding decrease in emphasis on the caring and comforting aspects of the profession. Meaningful communicative (verbal and non-verbal) interactions are apt to be neglected in the performance of additional administrative work, non-nursing, non-professional tasks or sophisticated technological nursing procedures.

Jourard (1966) reports how he spent two hours walking around a teaching hospital seeking episodes of body contact. He observed nurses and physicians tending to patients, relatives in conversation with patients: he patrolled corridors, watching interchanges between nurses and nurses, physicians and nurses, and physicians with each other. During that time two nurses' hands touched those of the patients to whom they were giving pills: one physician held a patient's wrist as he was taking a pulse and one intern placed his arm around the waist of a student nurse to whom he was engaged! 'Clearly,' he concludes, 'not much physical contact was in evidence.'

The nurse needs to develop a good patient-nurse relationship before touch can provide reassurance, comfort and support. Such a relationship also becomes a prerequisite for the patient to be comfortable with the nurse's use of touch. If the nurse is not in tune with herself and the patient she touches, physical intervention may prove inappropriate. Touching involves risk. By being authentic the nurse or carer can communicate her real intent. By reducing her distance with patients she can allow them to see her as one who is warm and concerned, yet competent. She must always bear in mind that individuals have thresholds of intimacy similar to thresholds of pain.

Durr (1971) interviewed both male and female medical-surgical patients to ascertain their recollections of and reactions to touch and closeness in relation to contacts with nurses. All the patients were convalescing but not completely recovered at the time of the interview. They tended to see physical contact as a means for both providing physical support and promoting understanding, and for verification of what the nurse was saying and feeling. Two female patients, one a 17 year old girl and the other a 60 year old woman, described recent situations in which they had experienced profound fear. Each looked to the nurse for comfort and security, and both experienced the belief that the *only* helping factor in relieving their fear was the nurse's touch. One patient remarked: 'Especially when a person is very ill, it helps you to know the nurse cares if she touches your arm or takes your hand.' A young patient, who believed she had been very ill, states: 'It's more encouraging if the nurse takes your arm when asking how you are, instead of standing at the foot of the bed.'

A 71 year old patient, immobilized by a fractured femur, was happy to remark after a rather disturbed night: 'In the morning one nurse stopped by my bedside. She just squeezed my hand and went back to work, but I knew that she remembered me from the day before and that she recognized that I was still a patient and still here – not forgotten.'

One patient when asked, 'Do you derive help when the nurse holds your hands?' replied: 'They don't do it very often.' Barnett (1972) claims that 'the act of touch is an integral part of nursing intervention and is to be used judiciously

51

between nurse and patients ... as a fundamental mechanic of communicating, a basis for establishing communication and as an important means of communicating emotions and ideas.'

A polio victim in his early sixties who had been in an iron lung for many years stated:

> Tactile contact is vitally important. People are so unconscious about touching. They touch something or someone every day, wherever they go. I finally realized why I had felt so lonely. It was because of my need to touch. I used to burst into tears [over this]. When someone touches me, it's like an electric shock that brings me out of that unusual lonely state. (Holbert, 1977)

Physical touch may well facilitate patient comfort and well-being, but the professional carer needs to know when, how, with whom and under what circumstances touch and personal distance are therapeutically relevant. In a study in the surgical area, Whitcher and Fisher (1979) carried out an experimental study to examine the effects on patients' psychological and physiological reactions when nurses held their hand during the pre-operative teaching session. The experimental manipulation took place after admission. The nurse touched the patient's hand for a few seconds while introducing herself and explaining that she was going to inform the patient about his or her surgery. Later the nurse put one hand on the patient's arm and maintained this touch for approximately one minute while she and the patient discussed a booklet that detailed the procedures for surgery. Patients in the control condition experienced the same interaction without physical contact. The results of the study indicated that female patients in the touched group experienced more favourable reactions than male patients in both groups and than females in the no-touch group. They experienced lowered anxiety, more positive feelings towards the nurses who used touch, together with more reciprocal touch and more favourable post-operative physiological responses (e.g. lower blood pressure).

The researchers concluded that the negative responses of male patients stemmed from their socialization against showing discomfort and dependency. The findings demonstrate that tactile stimulation in a hospital environment may sometimes be of therapeutic value. They also support those of Watson (1975) who found that men, except when under extreme stress, and the elderly, are less accepting than women of non-procedural touch by women.

While infants and young children are sick or hospitalized their need for comfort and security is exceedingly high. They depend on the touch of those who minister to them to sense that they are loved as well as to receive comfort. Intuitively we hug, kiss or pat the small child who grazes his knee even though the infant might be capable of accepting verbal comfort. Studies with sick children suggest that the child's sex may make a difference to the relief from stress acquired through physical touch. Newborn girls have been found to be more sensitive to touch than boys, but in early infancy boys receive more touch from their mothers (Westman, 1973), possibly because they are seen as being more irritable and fussier than girls (Moss, 1967). In Barnett's study (1972) of 540 patients, health personnel used touch 83 times with infants, 27 times with toddlers, 25 times with pre-school leavers and not at all with children 6 years and older. Tactile comfort can markedly minimize the distress exhibited by young children in hospital. In highly critical or emotional circumstances physical touch may be the only viable message of empathy that can be proffered. Wordless touch is not only reminiscent of maternal strokings but also basic to primate gestural language of affection and support.

For those who are acutely ill the nature of the hospital environment does much to determine responses to touch (see p. 42). In an article entitled 'Anatomy of an illness (as perceived by the patient)', Cousins (1976) noted 'the regularity with which hospital routine takes precedence over the rest requirements of the patient (slumber, when it comes for an ill person, is an uncommon blessing and is not to be wantonly interrupted), and over human aspects of care.'

The role of touch should not be overlooked in the care of the unconscious patient. In a lower level of consciousness a person may respond favourably to this basic and reassuring action of care-giving behaviour. It can be a mistake to consider the unconscious patient unable to hear or understand just because he has no subsequent memory on a conscious level. Some patients are able to recount their experiences when they regain consciousness. Physical touch can convey a willingness to help and the reassurance of the proximity of another person. Instances have been reported of touch stimulating a response from patients who otherwise failed to interact (Ashworth, 1980: Charles-Edwards, 1983). Unconscious patients can be restless and distressed when left alone and immediately become peaceful when someone is sitting with them.

Gesture and touch can give comfort to those patients who have lost the power of speech, such as stroke victims and those who have undergone major thoracic surgery. A graphic account of how meaningful communication was maintained with a 65 year old woman with right hemiplegia and aphasia (loss of speech) is given by Amacher (1973):

> Of all the interesting and rewarding experiences in working with Sally, the most important was learning to use touch therapeutically. Often, when we could not communicate verbally, I held her hand or hugged her around the shoulders to show I was trying to understand . . . I felt close to her, for touch involved me as no words could. Now, many months later, I often touch patients in greeting, and do not hesitate to touch them during treatments or examinations of their skin. I feel that touch often reassures patients who have had mutilating surgery that they are still loveable despite their deformities.

When a patient is deprived of speech he becomes isolated and alone without the means to reach out or make his needs known.

Touch has special relevance in the care of those who are suffering as a result of HIV viral infection. Many feel isolated and abandoned, and need to be assured that they are acceptable and 'touchable'. During the initial onset of the AIDS outbreak even a semi-official handshake from a member of the royal family or from a government minister did much to explode many of the myths surrounding the disease and to destigmatize those who suffer from it. One such patient remarked: 'To be touched by a fellow human – whoever it might be – helps me to feel I am still a person, not some leper or outcast branded with the letters AIDS!'

It is interesting to note the significance of tactile communication in the doctor-patient relationship. As physical touch is an important aspect of close, personal relationships, so it is essential in the formation of effective doctor-patient encounter. It forms part of everyday clinical skills from the initial handshake to heart massage. 'Through touch,' states an opthalmologist, 'I transmit my desire for the patient to get well. Even if it's nature that is the ultimate healer, your touch tells patients that you're on their side, that you're rooting for them to get well' (Older, 1982).

Trust plays an important part in the doctor-patient relationship: without it healing is unlikely to occur. Illness and helplessness are often intertwined and require compassion and understanding. There is a healing force present in every patient and a healing power present in a trusting relationship between patient and doctor. Hippocrates himself speaks of this: 'Some patients, though conscious that their condition is perilous, recover their health simply through their contentment with the goodness of the physician.' There is great need for the physician to be in actual touch with his patient. Increasing technology is no substitute for a thorough physical examination where the patient is touched and understood. A wise caution is given by the distinguished scientist Bronowski in his *The Ascent of Man* (1973): 'We have to cure ourselves of the itch for absolute knowledge and power. We have to close the distance between the press-button order and the human act. We have to touch people.'

A clinical examination is now mainly conducted by the use of instruments and touching of a patient by a physician has been minimized. This has prompted Older (1982) to ask whether 'human contact is always mediated through the steel of the stethoscope, the wood of the tongue depresser or the rubber of the patella hammer?' He also observes that 'if you examine people – and that means touching them – they'll often open out and tell you things that they quite clearly wouldn't have told you beforehand.' The simple act of pulse-taking can affect the heart, reduce shock and calm trauma victims (see p. 82). When a doctor touches a patient both parties have the 'feeling' that something is being done. There is much curative value in the 'bedside manner'. 'The reassurance of the softly spoken word, the confident touch of the hand that takes the pulse or taps the chest or turns the head to examine eyes and mouth, these are the body-contact actions that, for some, are better than a hundred pills' (Morris, 1971).

It was noted by Laycock almost a century and a half ago that there were instruments to aid the sense of vision (the microscope) and hearing (the stethoscope), but no aid for the sense of touch. He stressed the importance of touch in the first general examination of patients. Bruhn (1978) records that most people visit a physician when they are ill; they expect the physician to help them get well. Others visit physicians when they are troubled or worried about their real or imagined illnesses or those of relatives or friends; their expectation is that the physician will talk, listen, give advice, relieve feelings of fear or frustration or reassure them perhaps by a touch. A small number of people visit physicians periodically to check on their state of health; they hope the physician will give them 'a clean bill of health' and a pat on the back (i.e. a form of blessing), or will advise them of aspects of their health that warrant close scrutiny, i.e. a form of therapy or preventive medicine.

All three groups of patients expect some form of healing or laying on of hands by the physician. Thus, he concludes, while touching has diagnostic value for the physician touching also has therapeutic value for the patient.

> The quality of health care depends not only on how well physicians and other health professionals perform their tasks and the reliability of the technologies they use, but also on their ability to be human. To touch and be touched is part of the process of staying well or getting well.

Many physicians routinely shake hands with their patients while others consider taking a pulse as important for contact as it is for information. It is often during wordless periods of the palpating, probing and thumbing of a physical examination that the care-giving bond of doctor-patient relationship becomes established.

Modern medicine is often inclined to make the physician somewhat removed from the body. One doctor remarks: 'We've lost our skills of listening and touching. Instead we say we've no time, and order twenty-five tests on a patient without once touching him' (Curson, 1988). An older generation of general practitioners was more ready to:

> hold a patient's hand and say, 'Now tell me what's wrong with you, dear.' They open the door for patients to go out. They shake hands and pat hands when the patient enters the surgery. They place a hand on the knee that hurts and the belly that spasms. They pump the hand of the newly-fledged father . . . they sit in the old lady's armchair and drink her tea . . . they let each person know by tone of voice or action that they are welcome. . . .' (Heylings, 1973)

In most hospitals throughout the country there are hospital chaplains whose vocation lies in the pastoral care of the sick and of the members of staff who attend them. There are also parish priests and ministers who exercise an effective ministry to sick people who may be in their own homes, or in specialized units in the local community. Physical touch might be considered to be one of the most consciously neglected aspects of pastoral care of the sick, yet at the same time it is probably one of the most unconsciously used methods of expressing concern and compassion. Alongside other health personnel chaplains and local ministers touch those in their care without necessarily being aware of doing so. Tactile contact is, after all, a spontaneous gesture used often during pastoral conversation and in the more formal acts of 'blessing' and 'laying on of hands' (see p. 140). One patient (a priest himself) writes:

> . . . what interested me was what people did when they came [to visit me], especially my fellow priests . . . I was so grateful to the small number of priests who overcame their understandable shyness with a fellow-priest and laid hands on me and blessed me; and I knew which way I should decide in future when visiting sick people either at home or in hospital. . . . I believe that most of us, when we are sick, need physical contact and the spoken assurance of God's love. (Mayne, 1987)

Physical touch may be one of the chaplain's most valued 'tools' to help him fulfil his ministry in the midst of sick people. What happens in pastoral care depends not only on pastors caring but on how they *show* that care. Meaningful communication is conveyed not so much by words or deeds, important as they might be in given circumstances, but by the silent language of touch. While others come to sick beds to 'do something' the chaplain's ministry lies not so much in the realm of 'doing' as 'being'. Pastoral care of the sick is far more a function than an activity.

Touch is often a means of identifying with the patient, expressing 'alongsidedness' without appearing to patronize. It becomes meaningful when words are either not available or are transparently inadequate. No matter how experienced the professional carer may be in the art of communication there will always be occasions when the right words never seem to 'get across'. On such occasions as these, touch seems to say very much more than the best chosen words. Touch, too, can be seen as a mark of mutual trust and respect which leaves no place for deceit, lies or hypocrisy. It symbolizes shared humanity, equality, and can be a means of demonstrating the great deal that patients and those who care for them have in common. Far too frequently we erect barriers – verbal, emotional and psychological. If we are able to sit with our patients with a gentle hand on the arm, it says more than any words can that we see them as persons, fellow human-beings, in a crisis in which we are their friends as well as their comforters (Doyle, 1988).

Empathy is one of the most critical ingredients of the chaplain's helping relationship with the sick. It is the ability to enter into the life of another person; to view the world from the eyes of the other: to respond to the emotional content of another's communication, and to feel the pain and joy of the other. Such a spirit of empathy cannot be conveyed from a safe and secure distance from the bedside. To care means to be alongside the other, so that 'presence' becomes a 'healing presence'.

Touch enables the chaplain to be involved in the very existence and predicament of the sick person, helping to absorb the tensions, meanings and sufferings, often sharing in their very helplessness and despair. For:

> when we honestly ask ourselves which persons in our lives mean the most to us, we often find that it is those who, instead of giving much advice, solutions or cures, have chosen rather to share our pain and touch our wounds with

a gentle and tender hand. The friend who can be silent with us in a moment of despair or confusion, who can stay with us in an hour of grief and bereavement, who can tolerate not-knowing, not-curing, not-healing and face with us the reality of our powerlessness, that is the friend who cares. (Nouwen, 1974)

The chaplain is not there to 'stand off' and obscure in detachment, neither is he there to manipulate, dominate or control: he is there in silence often not knowing what to say but only knowing that he should be there, not afraid to hold a hand or even shed a tear.

By means of a comforting or reassuring touch a chaplain may enable a sick person to lower his defences and become increasingly open, revealing his deep anxieties, irritating doubts and crippling fears. During times of crisis many people have a tendency to withdraw. The chorus in T. S. Eliot's *Murder in the Cathedral* cry; 'Seven years we've lived quietly, succeeded in avoiding notice, living and partly living . . . but now a great fear is on us.' (Howe, 1963). Physical contact can encourage dialogue and give meaning to meeting.

Far too often has pastoral ministry to the sick become obsessed with words: 'What do I say?' 'Tell me what to say'. Little wonder sometimes we 'piggy-back on the trivial' as one patient so aptly described it. It is a mistaken concept which thinks that the mere desire to say something is enough. The 'silent' language of touch can be more important in a pastoral encounter than words, for 'much can be said without being spoken' (Nouwen, 1981).

Physical touch can be used effectively during moments of silence, prayer or pastoral conversation as well as in other circumstances of sickness described above. Such a gesture symbolizes friendship, acceptance and solidarity. However, like doctor or nurse, the chaplain too has to be aware that there will be some patients for whom physical touch is somewhat abhorrent. As with all who tend the sick, the priest or minister will bear in mind the maxim: 'To touch is not a technique: not touching is a technique!' (Older, 1977).

Abram, H. S.   'Psychological responses to illness and hospitalization', *Psychosomatics*, 10 (1969), pp. 218–224.

Amacher, N.   'Touch is a way of caring', *Amer. J. Nurs.*, (May 1973), pp. 852–854.

Ardrey, R.   *The Territorial Imperative*. Atheneum Publishers, New York 1966.

Barnett, K.   'A survey of the current utilization of touch by health team personnel with hospitalized patients', *Intern. J. Nurs. Studies*, 9 (1972), pp. 195–209.

Bettman, O. L.   *A Pictorial History of Medicine*. Charles C. Thomas, Springfield.

Bowlby, J.   'The nature of the child's tie to his mother', *Internat. J. Psychoanal.*, 39 (1958), pp. 350–373.

Bronowski, J.   *The Ascent of Man*. BBC Books, London 1973.

Bruhn, J. G.   'The doctor's touch: tactile communication in the doctor-patient relationship', *Southern Med. J.*, 71:12 (1978), pp. 1469–1473.

Charles-Edwards, A.   *The Nursing Care of the Dying Patient*. Beaconsfield Publ., Beaconsfield 1983.

Curson, R.   Quoted in 'Hands on heart', *Sunday Telegraph Magazine*. 8th May 1988.

Dominian, J.   'Psychological significance of touch', *Nursing Times*, 67:29 (1971), pp. 896–898.

Duff, R. S., and   *Sickness and Society*. Harper & Row, New
  Hollingshead, A. B.   York 1968.

Durr, C. A.   'Hands that help . . . but how?' *Nursing Forum*, X:4 (1971), pp. 393–400.

Farrah, S. J.   'The nurse's reported use of touch' (Unpublished Master's thesis of surgical nursing). University of Illinois (at the Medical Center) Chicago 1969.

Fromm, E.   *Human Dialogue*. The Free Press, New York 1957.

Goffman, E.   *Behavior in Public Places*. Free Press of Glencoe, New York 1963.

Goodykoontz, L.   'Touch: attitudes and practice', *Nursing Forum*, XVIII:1 (1979), pp. 4–16.

Henley, N. M.   'The politics of touch', in *Radical Psychology*, ed. P. Brown. Harper & Row, New York 1973.

Heyter, J.   'Territoriality as a universal need', *J. Adv.*
                           Nursing, 6 (1981), pp. 79–85.

Heylings, P. N. K.   'Personal view: the no touching epidemic –
                           an English disease', *Brit. Med. J.* (14 April
                           1973).

Holbert, D.   Quoted in *Nursing and the Aged*, ed. I. M.
                           Burnside. McGraw-Hill Book Co., New
                           York 1981.

Howe, R.   *The Miracle of Dialogue*. Seabury Press, USA
                           1963.

Huss, A. J.   'Touch with care or a caring touch?', 1976
                           Eleanor Clarke Slagle Lecture, *Amer. J. of*
                           Occupat. Therapy, 31:1 (1977), pp. 11–18.

Johnson, B. S.   'The meaning of touch in nursing', *Nursing*
                           Outlook, 13 (1965), pp. 59–60.

Jourard, S. M.   'An exploratory study of body-accessibility',
                           Brit. J. Soc. Clin-Psychol., (1966).

Langland, R. M., and 'Effects of touch on communication with
    Panicucci, C. L.   elderly confused clients', *J. Gerontological*
                           Nursing, 8:3 (1982), pp. 152–155.

Lamb, C.   *Essays*. Viking, New York 1949.

Laycock, T.   *Lectures on the Principles and Methods of*
                           Observation and Research. Blanchard & Lea,
                           Philadelphia 1857.

Lucente, F. E., and   'A study of hospitalization anxiety in 408
    Fleck, S.   medical and surgical patients', *Psychosomatic*
                           Med., 34 (1972), pp. 302–312.

Marsh, B. T.   'Be a patient', *Brit. Med. J.*, 295 (1987),
                           pp. 409–410.

May, R.   *The Meaning of Anxiety*. Ronald Press, New
                           York 1940.
                           Existence: A New Dimension in Psychiatry and
                           Psychology, eds. E. Angel and H. F.
                           Ellenberger. Basic Books, New York 1958.

McCorkie, R.   'Effects of touch on seriously ill patients',
                           Nursing Research, 23:2 (1974), pp. 125–132.

Mead, M.   'Nursing – primitive and civilized', *Amer. J.*
                           Nurs., 56:8 (1956), pp. 1001–1004.

Mercer, L. S.   'Touch: comfort or threat', *Perspectives in*
                           Psychiatric Care, 4 (1966), pp. 20–25.

Meredith, S.   'The importance of touch in patient care',
                           Imprint, 25 (1978), p. 66.

Minckley, B.	'Space and place in nursing care', *Amer. J. Nurs.*, 68 (1968), pp. 510–516.
Morris, D.	*Intimate Behaviour*. Book Club Assoc., London 1971.
Moss, A. A.	'Sex, age, and state as determinants of mother-infant interaction', *Merrill-Palmer Quarterly*, 13 (1967), pp. 19–36.
Nouwen, H.	*The Way of the Heart*. Darton, Longman & Todd, London 1982. *Out of Solitude*. Ave Maria Press, Notre Dame 1974.
Older, J.	*Touching is Healing*. Stein & Day Pub., New York 1982.
Walker, D. N.	'Openness to touching: a study of strangers in nonverbal interaction' (Doctoral Dissertation, University of Connecticut), *Dissertation Abstracts International*, 32 (1971), pp. 574. (University microfilms No. 71–18, p. 454).
Watson, W. H.	'The meanings of touch: geriatric nursing', *J. of Communication*, 25:3 (1975), pp. 104–112.
Westman, J. C.	*Individual Differences in Children*. Wiley, New York 1973.
Whitcher, S. J., and Fisher, J. D.	'Multidimensional reaction to therapeutic touch in a hospital setting', *J. Person. & Social Psychology*, 37:1 (1979), pp. 87–96.
Young, M.	'The human touch: who needs it?' in *Bridges not Walls: a book about Interpersonal Communication*, J. Stewart. Addison–Wesley Publ. Co. Inc., Massachusetts 1977.

4

Touch in Stress and Crisis Situations

But ah! the touch of lips and hands –
The human touch,
Warm, vital, close, life's symbol dear:
These need I most, and now and here.

     Richard Burton, 'Leaves of God'

'Crisis' and 'stress' are terms which cover a variety of meanings and are often used interchangeably. According to Rapoport (1962) the term 'stress' itself is used to denote three different sets of phenomena: (1) stress is equated with the stressful event or situation; (2) it is used to refer to the state of the individual who responds to the stressful event, and (3) more often stress refers to the relation of the stressful stimulus, the individual's reaction to it and the events to which it leads. The problem can be conceived of as a threat, a loss or a challenge. The ego tends to respond to each of these stages in a major characteristic mode. A threat to need and integrity, for example, is met with anxiety. Loss or deprivation is met with depression. If the problem is viewed as a challenge, it is more likely to be met with a mobilization of energy and purposive problem-solving activities. Lindemann and Caplan conceive of 'crisis' as the state of the reacting individual who finds himself in a hazardous situation. The following threatening events, or phases of crisis, are some examples in which the use of touch can exercise a therapeutic role.

PREMATURE BABIES

One acute emotional crisis situation described by Kaplan and Mason (1960) is the birth of a premature infant. A preterm baby is one who is born before 37 completed weeks of pregnancy. Kaplan delineates four normal psychological tasks that the mother must complete if she is to establish a healthy relationship with her premature infant. The primary task is preparation for the possible loss of the child whose life is at risk. 'Anticipatory grief' often involves emotional withdrawal from the infant as the mother simultaneously hopes for the babe's survival but prepares for his death. Another task is the mother's recognition and acknowledgement of her failure to deliver a normal full-term baby. When those first two tasks have been accomplished the mother then needs to resume the process of relating to the baby. Finally the mother must be able to recognize the special needs and requirements of a premature baby.

Premature babies are rather unusual patients, for the majority of such neonates are free of any organic pathology. They normally have to be cared for in neonatal intensive care units as they are helpless and cannot sustain their own basic life-support systems. As it is necessary for them to have highly technological nursing and medical care in such a specialized unit they have to be physically separated from their mothers, and so can be deprived of their consistent tactile contact.

An American undergraduate at Oxford recalls her experiences as a premature baby as well as her impressions of the need for touch. She was born 24 weeks after conception with a birth-weight of 2lb 3oz which later decreased to 1lb 12oz, and spent the first 2½ months of life in an incubator. Eventually she was discharged from hospital when she weighed 5lb.

She graphically describes those very early stages of life thus:

> I was totally alone. I yearned for some sort of tactile stimulus, but as I was laid on my back in the centre of the isolette the stimulus was minimal. At some point I discovered that I could change my position by wriggling, and that if I wriggled long enough I could eventually move myself into a corner. I remember ending up in the right-hand corner

nearest my head. I found that position comforting, because there I could touch two walls at once as well as the bottom of the isolette. I remember my frustration and desolation at being moved back into the centre by the two sets of gloved hands that reached me through the portals of the isolette. As many times as the hands moved me to the centre, I wriggled back into the corner. . . . I seem to have derived no comfort whatever from the touch of the gloved hands, perhaps because they thwarted my drive for solid, womb-like contact, or perhaps because latex is just not the same as real skin.

There appeared to be two possible side effects of her early isolation. 'First, I learned very quickly to differentiate between myself and the outside world. Thus from early on I've had a strong sense of my own personal and psychological boundaries, which has led me to make a firm demarcation of my own personal space. . . . Second, I revel in and thrive on affective touch. I love bearhugs. A good firm bearhug makes me feel loved and secure in a way nothing else can.'

In her early years, because of her spasticity, she was frequently touched by a variety of people.

I sensed instinctively the difference between clinical and affective touching, and remember being confused on the occasions when my parents used clinical touch to help me with my exercises. I wasn't able to articulate the difference until I was about 9 years of age, by which time I could intuit almost immediately in the course of an exploratory examination whether or not a particular practitioner would be good for me. Now I can tell by a handshake whether or not someone has 'good hands'.

One of her favourite doctors was her first paediatrician who worked with her from the beginning. 'His touch was one of the kindest I ever felt, because he managed to combine clinical objectivity with a good deal of affective concern. . . . In retrospect', she concludes, 'I think he must have been a devout Christian.'

Nearly a fifth of all newborn babies will spend some of their first hours or days in a neonatal unit. The majority will be nursed in incubators which for some will be their 'home' for several weeks. An incubator (or 'isolette' as they are rather graphically described in the USA) is by no means an ideal setting in which to develop a parental relationship. Some studies suggest that the fact of prematurity means that babies are deprived of the sensory stimulation they would have received in the uterus until term. A great variety of stimulation programmes have been devised to try and make good this supposed lack. For example, Wycombe General Hospital, High Wycombe, Bucks, has a purpose-built special infant care unit which prevents separation of mothers and their newborn infants. Most mothers are transferred to the special care baby unit direct from the delivery suite to ensure that, if possible, no separation from their babies takes place in the critical first minutes and hours after delivery. There are naturally exceptions; some mothers who, in their own medical interests, must be cared for on the wards and those who have had surgery, e.g. caesarean sections. Some of the mothers' rooms open directly into the special care unit so that parents can easily see or care for their infants. Mothers eat together, allowing time for sharing experiences and mutual support.

An editorial in the *British Medical Journal* (6 June 1970) stresses the need for close bonding between the mother and her premature baby;

> It may well be that the immediate post-partum period is the most important time for the initial contact between mother and child, as it is in animals. Many (but certainly not all) mothers feel the urge to have skin contact with the baby immediately he has been born; they think that it is important that they should be fully conscious . . . and they want to put the baby to the breast immediately.

It is considered important that intervention should involve parents as this is likely to help them into a relationship with their child. If one of the stroking or massage techniques is used, it should be the parents who do the touching.

The earlier a mother comes to the premature unit and touches her baby the more rapidly her own physical recovery from the pregnancy and birth seems to progress (Klaus and Kennell, 1982). The serious effects of maternal deprivation have been stated by Bowlby (1952): 'When deprived of maternal care, the child's development is almost always retarded – physically, intellectually and socially and . . . symptoms of physical and mental illness may appear.' Consequently, one of the aims of neonatal intensive care is to reduce the negative effects of deprivation: to help the preterm infants gain weight and grow to full-term size as soon as possible. Paediatricians have found that delicate premature babies need tactile contact, and parents are encouraged to touch their babies. Nursing staff stress the differences between their handling of the baby which is often associated with the painful or unpleasant, with the rhythmic and soothing touch of the parents. Care has to be taken that the mother's anxiety is not transmitted to the baby by her style or mode of touching or stroking. Premature babies need 'time out' from too much sensory stimulation and this may need to be discreetly explained to the parents. When an infant is born prematurely and is in a specialized unit the discrepancy between the real baby and the fantasized ideal is far greater and more difficult to resolve. In the place of positive emotions such as pride and joy, are feelings of guilt, anger and failure. Mothers fear that something they did or did not do during pregnancy affected the baby and produced the prematurity.

Benfield et al. (1976) in a survey of 101 parents in an intensive care unit documented the pervasiveness of parental grief that anticipated the death of their infant, even though the infant's life was not at risk. Other studies have shown how parental response is frequently one of over-protection, manifested by fears that the premature baby might stop breathing during the night. There is also concern with the child's weight gain, and anxiety about separation from the child. Current trials are being undertaken to investigate whether the holding of premature babies skin-to-skin has any positive benefits. Much has been learnt from the care of the new-born at San Juan de Dios Hospital, Bogota, Columbia, which has discharged back home babies weighing as little as 700g, cared for between the mother's breasts in a vertical position and fed on mother's milk ('kangaroo babies'). Infants as immature as 32 weeks gestation were successfully cared for at home in this way (Whitelaw and Sleath, 1985). The Bogota programme was supported by the United Nations Children's Fund (UNICEF) which reported (1983):

Instead of being placed in an incubator, low birth-weight babies are packed close to their mothers, right next to the breast. The new technique needs no technology and its cost is zero. Before the new techniques were introduced all babies weighing less than one kilo died. Now three quarters of them are being saved. For those weighing between 1000 and 1500 grammes the death rate has dropped from 70 per cent to 10 per cent.

It is important, however, to note that the premature babies placed skin to skin were in general very malnourished. They were mature and well developed (instead of being 27 weeks gestation they were probably 32–33). They appeared to be quite starved but did gain weight when placed close to the body of their mother.

In Britain babies are generally nursed in incubators until they are well over 3lb (1.4kg) and often do not go home until they are around 4lb (1.8kg). Whitelaw (1984) finds that the baby's temperature is steadier when it is held next to the mother's body than it is in an incubator. Babies also seem less restless when they are nursed in this way. 'We don't know why the baby is more contented next to the human body,' states Whitelaw, 'it could be the mother's heart-beat.' In Bogota mothers were also encouraged to massage gently the whole of the baby's body. Research conducted at Bedford College, London, demonstrates scientifically how massage can help premature babies. It has been found in experiments with more than 100 babies, mostly premature, that those who are stroked put on weight faster and develop more quickly.

Babies seem to enjoy being stroked and respond with 'purring' and stretching, and this helps to establish strong bonds between mother and baby. One of the nursing staff at the Hammersmith Hospital carries some of the premature babies around the ward with her, tied to her chest. She finds that it does not stop her from working with other sick babies on ventilators, and that the babies she carries around seem to be more contented than they are in an incubator (Gillie, 1984).

Research has described the difficulty parents have in relating to infants in neonatal intensive care units (Prugh, 1953:

Duhamel, 1974). It has been found that many mothers do not perceive the infant as their own until he is home. There is also the possibility that some mothers might accept their at-risk infants more readily if extended personal contact with the infant is delayed until he is healthier and more responsive. There are other mothers who may wish to see, touch, talk to and physically care for their babies as soon as possible.

In order to alleviate the stress of young babies who are being treated in a neonatal intensive care unit researchers are at present exploring various forms of soothing stimulation that might be applied. In one study by Field et al. (1986) premature neonates were provided with 45 minutes per day of stroking and passive movements of the limbs. The treatment group received tactile stimulation (stroking of the head and face region, neck and shoulders, back, legs and arms) for three 15 minute periods during three consecutive hours per day for ten days. These infants averaged 47% greater weight gain per day than the control group. Again, the infants in the treatment group were in hospital for six fewer days than the control infants. Such studies reveal that simple forms of tactile stimulation can help to alleviate the general stress of being in a neonatal intensive care unit, and also facilitate the clinical course of the premature infant.

Gottfried et al. (1981, 1984) conducted continuous 24 hour recordings of physical contacts between caregivers and premature infants in intensive care units during a typical day. The data revealed that such infants do not lack contact with people. They found that, on average, the infants received 70 contacts per day, with one infant receiving as many as 106. Infants in the neonatal convalescent care unit received 42 contacts per day with an upper limit of 55. Most contacts were only of a few minutes duration: there was no regularity or schedule involved. Although virtually all contact involved touching or handling, most of the handling may be appropriately described as non-social. Only 3% of the infants' contacts were with family members. These observational findings reveal that premature babies in special care units receive a considerable amount of handling per day, but that it is primarily the result of medical and nursing care. Social touching occurs infrequently.

One senior nurse of a special care baby unit records how

much touch matters in the care of the mothers of premature and very sick infants:

> Mothers respond so well to the touch of hands and to an arm around the shoulder, and at times a 'shoulder to cry on' . . . parental involvement is the key-note of our unit, so that they are touching and helping in the care of their premature sick baby from a very early stage. Breast feeding is encouraged even with the very sick infants. We are more and more placing babies between their mother's breasts for warmth, comfort and pleasure. (Macdonald, 1987)

The sources that may create stress for parents include the environmental stimuli, or the physical and psychosocial environment, the situational conditions and personal or family factors. A feeling of helplessness may be experienced as parents are unable to protect or hold their child. They have an intense need to be with the child, and as the child's condition improves the need becomes more urgent. Most parents usually feel comfortable reading a story, bathing, giving a back rub or feeding their child (Miles, 1979).

Another sister working in a neonatal unit tells how:

> even when the baby is very sick we encourage parents to carry out some of the caring procedures – many of which include touching i.e. nappy changing and cleaning the genital area, oiling the skin and cleaning the mouth.
>
> Once the baby's condition permits we allow and encourage parents to hold their baby whenever and for as long as they wish. Our aim is for parents to come into the unit and pick up the baby spontaneously from the incubator. They always check that it is in order to do this but they are not expecting help. Mothers enjoy the feeling (skin-to-skin) and most babies seem to. There seems to be no higher risk of infection for the babies and their temperatures remain well controlled even if they are very small and out of the incubator for some time. . . . Does all this touching help? I don't know how it would be possible to evaluate this objectively in an atmosphere where it is always actively encouraged. I feel that it can only be beneficial and most parents seem to appreciate and enjoy the encouragement to do these things. (Watson, 1988).

The differences in the effects of handling of premature babies by nurses and mothers was studied by Powell (1934), who found that infants who were handled by nurses had much more contact time (40 minutes per day). The infants in the group who received maternal handling were only handled during maternal visits every 4.8 days. Those infants who were handled by the nursing staff gained their birthweight back more quickly.

A senior nurse in a neonatal unit records:

> If possible, we involve both parents in the care of their baby. Initially we help them to have contact stroking, holding and talking to him ... if the mother is unwell every effort should be made to bring her to see the baby at the earliest opportunity ... we manoeuvre the bed close enough so that she is able to touch the baby. We remove the baby's gloves, bootees, cling film etc. and reassure the mother that baby needs her and knows that she is there. The nurse may need to show the mother what to do without making her feel self-conscious, by gently stroking the baby's arm or leg and talking at the same time ... with a little practice, staff can help parents to hold their baby, even if it is attached to monitors of all kinds. (Whitby, 1988)

Sometimes the combination of mechanical impediments to touching, and fear of inducing harm by touching, leads both doctors and nurses to minimize tactile contact with premature babies in special care baby units. When the condition of infants is stable, handling and rocking appear to be beneficial. There appears to be a marked difference between nursing procedural and non-procedural touch. The low frequency of non-procedural touch is noted by Blackburn and Barnard (1985) who reported that the mean number of loving touches was about five touches in a 24 hour period.

When a premature baby dies the parents' grief seems to last considerably longer if they have had no opportunity to handle and touch the infant. Where there has been tactile contact the parents appear to show a less extended period of disorganization. If they have been unable to touch the baby and so verify its existence they feel they have missed out on a very valuable experience. Mothers who wish to see their dead baby should be encouraged to touch, handle and fondle it in order to say a tactile farewell. It is never an easy decision for a mother to make. The procedure may seem strange to some parents, yet an obvious desire for others. The experience of holding a baby even though dead may make him a more real person to remember and in this way help both mother and father (Beard, 1978). In many units if the baby dies parents are encouraged to hold their baby after death for as long as they wish, thus letting death be seen as part of life. Some will wish to bathe and dress the baby. This procedure has been found to be very beneficial to most parents and they look back on it with positive feelings.

Klaus and Kennell (1976) quote some words of a mother who did not have the opportunity to touch her dead child:

> I didn't get a chance to really touch him, to hold him like a mother. This is something a mother wants to do so much, to touch the baby. Even though she knows she can't pick it up, she wants to touch it. Sometimes I dream about him, and I can see him, and I wake up. I didn't really pick him up. But the dreams go that I'm picking him up and holding him, and I know that I didn't do it. So I wake up because I wanted to so badly.

It is important, should the parents so desire, for them to have time with the body, to touch it and if necessary to weep over it; this is to have a time in which the death of the infant can become a reality.

Susan Hill (1989), the well-known novelist, whose baby daughter, Imogen, was born 15 weeks premature and weighed only 630 grams (less than 1½lb), describes how in the special care nursing she used to touch Imogen's hand, stroke her and feel her grip. As she stroked her baby's arm gently, the nurse in charge said: 'See, she knows you – her heart rate increases a bit when you first touch her, then it goes nice and steady.'

Later, when Imogen's condition unfortunately becomes critical and her eyes remain closed, the doctor on duty suggested that her mother held her – 'don't worry, I'm sure it'd be a good thing for you both.' As her very sick premature baby was lowered gently into her waiting arms, Susan Hill describes the experience:

> It was the most miraculous, most wonderful thing. And as

I held her, I felt her tense, taut little body relax and, for a moment, suddenly, her face twitched, twitched again – and then she opened her eyes, and I saw that brilliant blue, clouded, perhaps unseeing, but there. 'She likes that – look.' One of the sisters on duty was smiling, pointing to the monitor. 'She knows it's you. Look.' And, sure enough, her heart monitors were steady.

Imogen was to live for only five weeks, and when she eventually died, her mother sat for a long time holding her in her arms. At that moment of time death appeared to be 'the most important, the most significant thing in life'. Imogen's mother felt in awe of it and yet quite peaceful, as though she were in the company of a familiar friend. 'I was not afraid,' she writes, 'I did not recoil, and I wanted this time to last for ever, to hold on to it. Because here, now, I felt as if I were within reach of understanding the secret of the universe.'

INTENSIVE CARE UNITS

Another scene of crisis and stress is the intensive care unit. Paradoxically the atmosphere of an intensive care unit is both highly personal and impersonal. The patient is normally attached to technical apparatus: he is kept under constant surveillance, and the medical and nursing staff at his bedside make his care far more personal than that of the average hospital patient. Yet it is this concentrated attention and the equipment around him which can create for many a patient an impersonal environment in which he may experience a variety of emotional reactions. The scene has been set by Mayerson (1976):

> Monitors, respirators, suction devices and other bedside equipment; glaring lights, bleeps and oscillations; the hushed tones and scurrying of personnel; telephones ringing at the central station, the paging intercom; the starkness and sterility of the room; the turmoil of recurring emergency activities; and tubes in every available orifice provide ample ground upon which this variety of feelings can develop.

As the world of health is a social world, the enforced inactivity, passivity and dependence can cause a sense of personal annihilation, which alone is enough to create depression and anxiety. While most patients find the atmosphere reassuring rather than menacing, some may experience depression and distress because of sensory monotony and sleep deprivation. One of the major difficulties faced by patients centres around the depersonalizing and dehumanizing aspect of intensive care experience. In such an environment the importance of communication cannot be over-emphasized:

> Perhaps the single most important suggestion we could make is that helping professionals be willing communicators with patients. For the supine patient caught in a situation of near helplessness, communication is about the only mode of activity through which he can affect his environment and work out suitable coping strategies . . . we suggest greater emphasis on listening to the patient and responding to his cues . . . such an approach to communication may require practice, but its results are well worth the effort. (Garrity and Klein, 1975)

To respond and do things meaningful to patients requires understanding and appreciating what is meaningful to them. As many intensive care patients are artificially ventilated and therefore unable to speak normally, verbal communication is extremely difficult. A total of 106 out of 112 nurses from five intensive care units found it difficult at times to understand what their patients wanted to say (Ashworth, 1980). Even though the patient appears unconscious there may be physiological reactions to psychological stimuli. One patient who was unconscious and on a ventilator has described her anxieties and fears from not being able to communicate:

> I was unconscious as far as the medical staff were concerned, but I could hear. I knew I was on a ventilator. I could not move or do anything, but I could hear. They were talking about me. I wanted to communicate in some way. I tried desperately to move a finger, blink an eyelid or do something to let them know that I was there . . . to them [the staff] I was unconscious. But I can remember whole conversations . . . since then I have recounted con-

74

versations to staff concerned, to their surprise, and they have confirmed my accuracy. (Boon, 1983)

Many patients who undergo intensive treatment for critical physical conditions appear to develop considerable sensitivity to what is happening around them.

A number of patients depend heavily on non-verbal signals such as tone of voice or physical touch. McCorkle (1974) notes how touching and talking to seriously ill patients indicates concern for them. It symbolizes a presence with them, and they appreciate knowing someone 'is there'. Henderson (1966) suggests that the nurse should become the 'consciousness of the unconscious'. Tactile communication can convey the reassuring message: 'I care, I'm here, you're safe.'

A lecturer in a Department of Nursing Studies records her experiences of three days spent in 'intensive care' in a southern Swiss hospital after sustaining a major head injury:

It surprised me how much I valued human touch. I wanted my hand held by everyone – doctors, nurses, visitors. The doctors had no difficulty in meeting this need, since it is customary for Swiss people to shake hands on meeting and parting. The nurses, however, although also Swiss and extremely friendly, behaved much more like the undemonstrative British and did not use touch. How sad and serious if they lose this natural asset during their nursing training. (Redfern, 1985)

Another patient recalls her experience of being ventilated:

I longed for those firm but gentle hands to lift, turn and support my body. I ached to be moved, but when I felt them and heard the simple explanations, the time, the date and that I was going to be OK, I knew I was safe. (Mackereth, 1987)

A nurse in a surgical intensive care unit describes what touch meant to one of her patients:

When I saw the mental anguish this man was suffering I took his hand and slowly told Jerry many of the things he should have already been told ... as we talked his face brightened and I could see his tense little body relaxing ... how many times we assume that our patients know exactly what is happening and miss their mental anguish because it is so easy for us to get caught up in other aspects of care. (Barker, 1988)

Barnett (1970) observed that patients in good and fair conditions are touched 20 per cent more often than acutely ill patients. She suggests that the seriously ill patient is touched less partly because 'health team members have a fear of death and find it difficult to provide the emotional support necessary', and partly because the 'personnel are often so busy with the technical aspects of stabilizing the patient's condition that there is not enough time to provide the emotional support necessary.'

The carer needs to be sensitive and receptive, and able to interpret non-verbal communication. It is suggested by Bowlby (1958) that in situations of danger, crisis and incapacity the adult's need for tactile communication increases. It is the perception of the situation, not the situation itself, which induces stress. Stressors in an intensive care environment include mechanical ventilation, the frightening atmosphere, lack of sleep, noise and feeling tied down by equipment (de Meyer, 1967: Ballard, 1981). The loneliness and monotony are well illustrated in some words of reflection by a former intensive care patient:

Morning, evening
here and now
co-mingle with eternity.
Moments merge to haunting hours, never ending flow of days,
time becomes a shadowed clock.

Problems in communication appear to be a major source of inter-personal stress. One patient stated that it was 'the biggest problem about being on the respirator'. Such inability to communicate has been described by patients in the following terms: 'I couldn't make them understand anything', 'You try and talk and nothing comes out'; 'It was depressing' (Gries and Fernsler, 1988). In a study of 'hand-holding' with critically ill patients in an intensive care unit, undertaken by Knable (1981), several nurses claimed touch in the form of hand-holding really made them 'want to help the patient'. In addition, it 'seemed to break down barriers'. Nurses also claimed hand-holding was visibly beneficial to the patient. Several patients who were moaning in apparent discomfort appeared more comfortable for as long as 30 minutes after hand-holding. After some of the nurses had terminated their tactile contact, a number of patients were seen to reinstate it. Hand-holding obviously had a soothing effect, reduced anxiety and increased the patient's sense of security.

A patient who spent 18 days in an intensive care unit with post-surgery complications and respiratory problems recalls her experiences:

> How grateful I was to those perceptive nurses who paused to wipe me dry with sterile gauze pads . . . understanding, concern, empathy – these essential qualities could never be communicated by impersonal machines, no matter how streamlined their construction. . . . Almost any weekday morning our ward overflowed with aides, technologists, nurses, doctors . . . yet even with dozens of persons scurrying about the relationships could be impersonal. In contrast to the cold steel of my respirator or transparent glass of my suction jar, I wanted the touch of a warm, human hand. Dr S.'s ventilation meter could measure my lung capacity, but no instrument could evaluate my gratitude to the nurse who smiled at me as she mopped my face. . . . (Carlson, 1968)

These comments from both nursing staff and patients are supported in part by Schmahl (1964): 'Through touching the patient, the nurse can convey to him her gentleness, her feeling of caring for him, her understanding of his feelings.'

CORONARY CARE UNITS

The psychological care of patients in coronary care units has not received a great deal of attention. Admission to a coronary care unit after suffering a heart attack naturally results in a very stressful situation for the patient and his family. Various studies have found that patients with myocardial infarction are extremely anxious on admission and for the first 48 hours, but anxiety seems to decrease throughout their stay in hospital (Philip et al., 1979). According to Lazarus (1966) the following stimuli produce stress: uncertainty about physical survival; threat to identity; separation or loss of loved ones; inability to control one's own environment; disruption of community life, and pain or deprivation. All these conditions are applicable to a patient on admission to a coronary care unit. Pain is often of a severe nature, may last for several hours and may also interfere with breathing. This in itself can be an extremely stressful experience. To suffer a myocardial infarction for the first time reminds the patient that life is finite and the future uncertain (Benoliel and Velde, 1975).

Some research has been carried out on the effect of touch on patients in a coronary care unit, but with rather inconsistent results. It has been suggested by Weiss (1986) that the confusion arises on account of the different types of touch in use (procedural, and comforting or reassuring). Most often, whereas procedural touch can result in further stress, comforting touch has a relaxing effect. 'Different types of touch may have varying psychological and social implications. In addition the skin is a highly complex and versatile organ, with an immense range of psychologic operations and a wide repertoire of responses' (Weiss).

Management of the nature of caregiver touch may significantly contribute to the well being of a coronary care patient. In the coronary care unit most touching is either task-orientated or it strives to comfort the patient. Various studies reveal that in general caregivers are rather uncomfortable touching patients (Burton and Heller, 1964: Huss, 1977). 'Comforting touch' has been described by Morse (1983) as one involving empathy or the acute awareness of the feelings and emotional needs of the person being touched. It is touch expressing concern or involvement, with the intent of being perceived as reassurance, caring, pain relieving and comfort giving.

Research has also indicated physiologic factors as crucial predictors of the effect of touch. For example, Lynch et al. (1974) has shown how the laying of the nurse's hand on the unconscious patient can bring about slowing of the patient's heart-rate even while undergoing tracheal suctioning. They record how the most universally recognized aspect of bedside manner is the ability of the physician and other medical personnel to influence the measurement of blood pressure, heart-rate and other variables of cardio-vascular performance.

They have described the effects of human contact on the cardiac response of patients in coronary care units, where even the simple act of taking the pulse produces significant changes in heart-rate. The authors quote Celsus (c. AD 30), one of the most famous Roman medical scribes, on the art of pulse-taking in his *De Medicina*:

> On the contrary, bathing, exercise, fear and anger, and any other state of mind, may often be apt to excite the pulse, so that when the medical man first comes, the anxiety of the patient, who is in doubt as to what he may seem to him to have, may upset the pulse. For this reason, it is not the part of an experienced doctor that he seize the arm with his hand at once; but first of all sit down with a cheerful expression and enquire how he feels, and if there is any fear of him, to calm the patient with agreeable talk: and then, at last, lay his hand on the patient's body. How easily a thousand things may disturb the pulse, which even the sight of a doctor may upset!

One type of interaction studied was planned interaction in which one of the two graduate nurses, who was aware of the purpose of the study, either took the patient's pulse, or held the patient's hand or touched his arm. The nurse then verbally comforted him with the following type of statement:

> (First name of patient), my name is (first name of nurse) and I am a nurse. I know you can't answer me when I talk to you even though you can hear me. That's because of your medication ... there is a machine at your bedside breathing for you which you may be able to hear. This medicine is an unpleasant but very necessary part of your treatment so please try and relax and bear with it ... we will try to anticipate your needs since you are presently unable to communicate them to us. There is always a doctor or nurse at your bedside so please try not to worry.

The study examined the effects of human contact on the heart-rate of four seriously injured patients who were artifically respirated. All four patients showed significant heart-rate change during routine clinical interactions such as pulse-taking or when a nurse held their hand and comforted them.

Lynch (1977) also showed that heart-rate and frequency of

cardiac arrhythmias decreased when a nurse remained in a patient's room longer than five minutes. However, when the nurse stayed less than five minutes in the room and had no human contact with the patient, the monitor showed increased heart rate and cardiac arrhythmias (see Figures 1 and 2, pp. 81 and 82).

Such studies reveal how simple quiet comforting by a nurse can significantly alter the patient's heart-rate and influence the frequence of arrhythmia (i.e. any variation from the normal rhythm of the heart beat). In an age of automated patient-care, touch can often be the critical human dimension in machine-orientated care. Touch can provide that special dimension in care which sustains the patient through a time of profound stress and anxiety.

It is interesting to note that analogous cardio-vascular effects of human contact have been described in animal studies. In both dogs and horses various types of routine human contact can produce gross changes in heart-rate, blood pressure and coronary flow (Newton and Gantt, 1968). When a human pets a dog usually an abrupt bradycardia (slowness of the beating of the heart with corresponding slowness of the pulse) is elicited.

A Religious who works in a hospice records the following beneficial effect of touch on the heart-rate:

> I sat by a young girl critically ill and deeply unconscious with meningitis and encephalitis. Her heart beat was monitored and was extremely rapid. As we [her mother and I] sat by her bedside, we stroked her arm. Gradually, the rate of heart beat decreased. When we stopped stroking her a few moments later, it increased again slightly, but not as high as it had been. The story has a happy end, for she has made a remarkable recovery and there is virtually no residual damage.

Touch when introduced consciously and appropriately into the nurse-patient relationship may therefore facilitate the process of communication, show changes in heart-rate and rhythm, as well as decrease levels of anxiety and reinforce a component of security and warmth in medical and nursing interaction. Lynch (1978) states that 'human contact seems to be desperately important to patients in these acute clinical

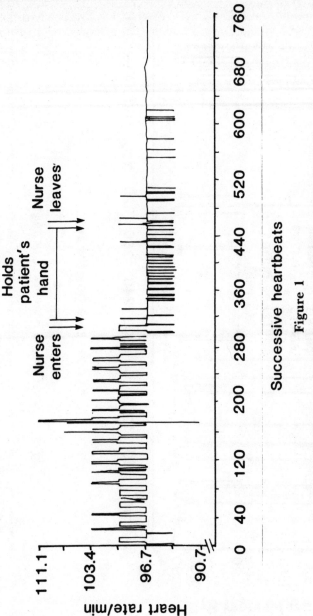

Heart rate/min

111.1 — 103.4 — 96.7 — 90.7

Nurse enters | **Holds patient's hand** | **Nurse leaves**

0   40   120   200   280   360   440   520   600   680   760

Successive heartbeats

Figure 1

Effect of Human Contact on Heart-Rate of Comatose and Curarized Man

Beat-to-beat heart-rate of patient before, during and after nurse holds patient's hand and comforts him. Note decrease in heart-rate and stabilizing of heart rhythm during and after nurse's contact with patient. For the three minutes before the nurse came to his bedside, the patient had not been approached by any other medical staff.

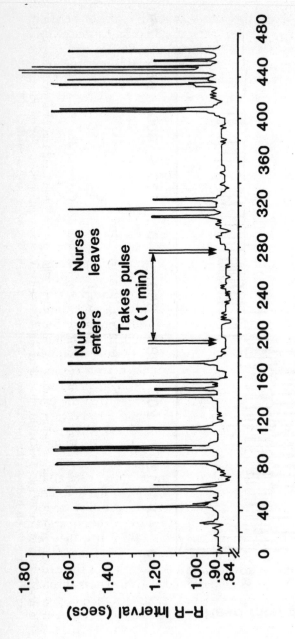

Figure 2

Effect of Pulse-Taking on Heart-Rate After Atropine Therapy

Beat-to-beat heart-rate of patient before, during, and after pulse-taking. Note the elimination of intermittent heart block during pulse taking. Heart-rate and rhythm were normal during pulse-taking.

settings, and, in these environments, the heart seems almost hyper-reactive to even the most ordinary types of personal contact.' In studying nurse-patient communication within intensive care Ashworth (1980) found that 85 per cent of the nurses interviewed felt that they would use touch to convey reassurance, comfort and security to the patients.

FAMILIES

They suffer most who stand and stare
the helpless lovers yearning to absorb the pain
or bear the threat of lifelessness.
Friends and families long to comprehend the grim event
yet never can incorporate the solitude of patienthood.

So wrote a patient who had spent some time in an intensive care unit and who was very much aware of those around her. Admission to an intensive or coronary care unit can create enormous anxiety and stress for both patient and family. They initially feel shock, fright, disbelief and numbness. Some may feel guilty about their anger at the patient for being ill or guilty for wishing the patient would die. In interviews with wives of 65 patients who had been admitted to a coronary care unit feelings of grief, guilt and over-protectiveness were highlighted. Breu and Dracup (1978) observed that the partners of coronary care patients were grieving for the loss of their loved one before the actual death. Such an awareness of the likelihood of death is described by Hampe (1975) as 'an anticipatory grief'.

Families and relations have to relinquish their care-giving role and are reduced to the status of visitors. Their feelings of helplessness and inadequacy make them feel guilty, reducing them from having value to vulnerability (Gibbon, 1988). Intimidated by all the equipment, tubes and drips, they feel compelled to remain aloof, unable to talk to or touch the patient. Under such circumstances it is essential for the carers to convey a sense of personal psychological closeness through empathy, respect and compassion. The significance of physical touch as well as conveying to the patient support and orientation will also give the family members reassurance and security.

Lust (1984) identified the essence of total patient-care as effective communication among nurse, patient and family, and stressed the importance of the inclusion of the family into the environment of the intensive care. Family members particularly note such nursing gestures as calling their patient by name, stroking him, and whenever practical allowing them to hold his hand and be as near as possible to him. They may reach to touch him but find they are often hesitant and fearful because of all the tubes and equipment. The nursing staff need to assess the family's readiness to touch the patient, and to let them know when it is in order to do so.

When the patient is a child the family may be allowed to involve themselves in his care by doing such things as stroking him and/or feeding him. Parental feelings at a time of crisis are not static but are constantly changing, and among the major stresses of an intensive care unit is the change in their role and relationship with their child. Nursing assessment and intervention will help to reinforce positive coping in parents by providing adequate information and helping them to find the resources to meet their needs.

Ashworth, P. 'Care to communicate – an investigation of communication between patients and nurses in intensive therapy units', series ed. F. S. Beck. Royal College of Nursing, London, 1980.

Ballard, K. 'Identification of environmental stressors for patients in a surgical intensive care unit', *Issues Ment. Health Nurs.*, 3 (1981), pp. 89–108.

Barker, R. K. 'You made a difference', *Focus on Critical Care*, 15:2 (1988), p. 38.

Barnett, K. E. 'The development of a theoretical construct of the concepts of touch as they relate to nursing' (Unpublished doctoral dissertation). North Texas State University, Denton, Texas 1970, p. 87.

Beard, F. W.   'Help for parents after stillbirth', *Brit. Med. J.* (21 Jan 1978), pp. 172–173.

Benoliel, J. Q., and Van de Velde, S.   'As the patient views the intensive care unit and coronary care unit', *Heart & Lung*, 4 (1975), pp. 260–264.

Benfield, D. G., et al. 'Grief response to parents after referral of the critically ill newborn to a regional center', *New Eng. J. Med.*, 294 (1976), pp. 975–978.

Blackburn, S. N., and Barnard, K. E.   'Analysis of caregiving events in preterm infants in the special care unit', in *Infant Stress under Intensive Care*, eds A. W. Gottfried and I. Gaiter. University Park Press, Baltimore, 1985, pp. 113–119.

Boon, S.   'A pawn in a chess game', *Nursing Mirror* (26 October 1983), pp. 29–30.

Bowlby, J.   *Maternal Care and Mental Health* (2nd ed.). World Health Organisation, Geneva 1952. (Monograph Series No. 2.)
'The nature of a child's tie to his mother', *Int. J. Psychoanal.*, 39 (1958), pp. 350–373.

Breu, D., and Dracup, K.   'Helping the spouse of critically ill patients', *Amer. J. Nurs.*, 78 (1978), pp. 50–53.

Burton, A., and Heller, L. G.   'The touching of the body', *Psychoanal. Review*, 5 (1964), pp. 122–134.

Carlson, D.   *The Unbroken Vigil: Reflections on Intensive Care*. John Knox Press, Richmond, Virginia 1968.

de Meyer, J.   'The environment of the intensive care unit', *Nurs. Forum*, 6 (1967), pp. 262–272.

Duhamel, T. R., et al. 'Early parental perceptions and the high risk neonate', *Clin. Pediatrics*, 13:12 (1974), pp. 1052–1056.

Field, T. M., et al.   'Tactile/kinesthetic stimulation effects on preterm neonates', *Pediatrics*, 77 (1986), pp. 654–658.

Garrity, T. F., and Klein, R. F.   'Emotional response and clinical severity as early determinants of 6-month mortality after myocardial infarction', *Heart & Lung*, 4 (1975), pp. 730–737.

Gibbon, B.   'Stress in relatives', *Nursing*, 28 (1988), pp. 1026–1028.

Gillie, O.

In 'Nestling into life', *Sunday Times Supplement* (1984), pp. 17–21.

Gottfried, A. W.

'Environmental manipulations in the neonatal period and assessment of their effects', in *New-borns and Parents*, V. L. Smeriglio. Hillsdale, Erlbaum, New Jersey 1981.

'Infant stress under intensive care', *Environmental Neonatology*. University Park Press, Baltimore 1984.

Grant, G. P.

State of the World's Children. Oxford Univ. Press, London 1984.

Gries, M. L., and Fernsler, J.

'Patient perceptions of the mechanical ventilation experience', *Focus on Critical Care*, 15:2 (1988), pp. 52–59.

Hampe, S. P.

'The needs of the grieving spouse in a hospital setting', *Nursing Research*, 24 (1975), pp. 113–120.

Henderson, V.

The Nature of Nursing. The Macmillan Co., New York 1966.

Hill, Susan

Family. Michael Joseph, London 1989.

Huss, A. J.

'Touch with care or a caring touch' (1976 Eleanor Clarke Slagle Lecture) *Amer. J. Occup. Therap.*, 31:1 (1977), pp. 11–18.

Kaplan, D. M., and Mason, E.

'Maternal reactions to premature birth viewed as acute emotional disorder', *Amer. J. Orthopsychiatry*, 39 (1960), pp. 539–552.

Klaus, M. H., and Kennell, J. H.

Maternal-Infant Bonding. Mosby, St Louis 1976.

'Interventions in the premature nursery: impact on development', *Ped. Clinics N. Amer.*, 5 (1982), pp. 1263–1273.

Knable, J.

'Handholding: one means of transcending barriers of communication', *Heart & Lung*, 10 (1981), pp. 1105–1110.

Lazarus, R. S.

Psychological Stress and the Coping Process. McGraw-Hill, New York 1966.

Lindemann, E., and Caplan, G.

'A conceptual framework for preventive psychiatry', Unpublished paper.

Lynch, J. J., et al.

'The effects of human contact on cardiac arrythmia in coronary care patients', *J. Nerv. Ment. Dis.*, 158:2 (1974), pp. 88–99.

'Effects of human contact on the heart activity of curarized patients in a shock-trauma unit', *Amer. Heart J.*, 88:2 (1974), pp. 160–168.

'The simple act of touching', *Nursing*, 8 (1978), pp. 32–36.

Lust, B.   'The patient in the intensive care unit: a family experience', *Crit. Care Quarterly* (March 1984), pp. 49–57.

Macdonald, J.   Personal communication (1987).

Mackereth, P. A.   'Communication in critical care areas: competing for attention', *Nursing*, 15 (1987), pp. 575–578.

Mayerson, E. W.   *Putting the Ill at Ease.* Harper & Row, New York 1976.

McCorkle, R.   'Effects of touch on seriously ill patients', *Nursing Research*, 23:2 (1974).

Miles, M. S.   'Impact of the intensive care unit on parents', *Issues Compr. Pediatr. Nursing*, 3 (1979), pp. 72–90.

Morse, J. M.   'An ethnoscientific analysis of comfort: a preliminary investigation', *Nurs. Papers*, 15:6 (1983).

Newton, J. E. D., and Gantt, W. H.   'The history of a catatonic dog', *Conditional Reflex*, 3 (1968), pp. 45–61.

Philip, A. E., et al.   'Short term fluctuations in anxiety in patients with myocardial infarction', *J. Psychosomat. Research*, 23 (1979), pp. 277–280.

Powell, L. F.   'The effect of stimulation and maternal involvement on the development of low birth-weight infants and on maternal behaviour', *Child Development*, 45 (1974), pp. 106–113.

Prugh, D.   'Emotional problems of the premature infant's parents', *Nursing Outlook*, 1 (1953), pp. 461–469.

Rapoport, L.   'The state of crisis: some theoretical considerations', *Social Service Review*, 36 (1962), pp. 211–217.

Redfern, S.   'Taking some of my own medicine', *Care of the Critically Ill*, 1:5 (1985), pp. 6–7.

Schmahl, J. A.	'Ritualism in nursing practice', *Nursing Forum*, 11 (1964), p. 74.
Watson, S.	Personal communication (1988).
Weiss, S. J.	'Psychophysiologic effects of caregiver touch on incidence of cardiac dysrhythmia', *Heart & Lung*, 15:5 (1986), pp. 495–506.
Whitby, C.	'Caring for parents with a baby receiving intensive care', *Care of the Critically Ill*, 4:2 (1988), pp. 24–25.
Whitelaw, A., and Sleath, K.	'Myth of the marsupial mother: home care of very low birthweight babies in Bogota, Columbia', *The Lancet* (25 May 1985).
Whitelaw, A.	In 'Nestling into life', *Sunday Times Supplement* (1984), pp. 17–21.

5

Touch in Counselling and Psychotherapy

To touch is not a technique: not touching is a technique.

J. Older, 'Touching is Healing' (1982)

The two terms, counselling and psychotherapy, are sometimes used synonymously, but normally counselling would refer to those procedures employed to help people who have personal problems which they feel are beyond self-solution. Psychotherapy delves deeper, often into the unconscious and the collective unconscious, while counselling confines itself to the conscious. The methods of both are often similar, and it is essential for the counsellor to have knowledge and understanding of the principles of psychotherapy.

In his early work on hysteria Freud (1957) was impressed by the apparent power of touch in assuaging patients who were distraught. During some sessions in his practice he stroked the patient's head or neck for stimulative effect, and also allowed patients to touch him. He wrote:

I decided to start with the assumption that my patients knew everything that was of pathogenic significance, and it was only a question of obliging them to communicate it. Accordingly, when I asked the question: 'What is the origin of your symptom?' and received the answer: 'I don't know', I took the patient's head between my hands and said, 'You will think of it under the pressure of my hands – at the moment I relax my pressure, something will come into your head. Catch hold of it.' I was surprised to find that it yielded the precise results which I needed. . . . Eventually, I grew so confident that, if the patient answered: 'I see nothing', I dismissed it as impossible and assured him that he certainly had become aware of what was wanted, but had rejected it. (Cohen, 1969)

In his later publications, however, references to physical contact appear to be extremely rare or occasionally tabooed. He finally rejected physical contact, and condemned as seductive and dangerous Ferenczi's use of it (Jones, 1955).

Over the years as the art of psychotherapy evolved there were many clinicians who considered touch to be detrimental to the therapeutic relationship, and there are few references to touch in psychoanalytical texts and none to it as a part of technique. Two main reasons for the omission appear to be those of human frailty and the fear of sexuality, and the changes in the theories and techniques of psychoanalysis. At the turn of the century these changes chiefly centred round the discovery of transference and the principle of abstinence – the non-gratification of needs by the analyst. The analytical procedure was to act as a frustrater of needs and not to be a source of gratification which may have perpetuated the neurosis. These however cannot be seen as solely theoretical reasons for the taboos as they also reflect fears of sexual stimulation (Mintz, 1969).

A diversity of opinion has emerged in psychological literature concerning the use of touch. Wolberg (1954) and Menninger (1958), for example, absolutely forbade any touch in therapy for fear that it might arouse sexual feelings or bring forth outbursts of anger. Indeed, the latter went as far as to consider any physical contact on the part of the therapist as incompetent and 'criminal ruthlessness'. Wolberg states that 'it goes without saying that physical contact with the patients is absolutely taboo'.

More recent literature on touch in psychotherapy confirms the controversy and does little to clarify the issue. Very little appears to be known about how tactile contact may affect the feelings and behaviour of clients. One of the reasons for the lack of research may stem from ambivalent opinions concerning the use of touch in the therapeutic context. Although most therapists maintain a conservative bias against touching, only a relative few would today regard it as an absolute taboo. Perhaps the most significant use for physical touch in our context is its potential to encourage self-disclosure, which has been described as the key to inter-personal relationships (Jourard, 1964). Self-disclosure plays a significant role in psychotherapy where the essential elements are honest intro-spection and self-acceptance.

Pattison (1973), who was the first to report on the impact of touch in counselling, found that clients who were touched engaged in more self-exploration than did clients who were not touched. He contended that within the context of present-day therapeutic practice, tactile communication is assuming an ever-increasing role: there is a growing awareness that often a single touch seems to evoke an atmosphere of accept-ance and caring. Pattison's study and investigation dealt specifically with three questions: (a) do clients who are touched engage in more self-exploration than clients who are not touched? (b) are counsellors perceived differently by cli-ents they touch than by clients they do not touch, and (c) do counsellors feel different towards clients they touch than towards clients they do not touch?

A significant difference was found in self-exploration between clients who were touched and those who were not touched. Touch appeared to make no significant difference to counsellors' and clients' perceptions of relationship conditions offered by the counsellor in an initial interview. In the study counsellors reported in several cases feeling closer rapport with clients whom they touched. This result adds support to Jourard's findings (1968) that self-disclosure and touching are correlated. He noted that 'some form of physical contact with patients expedited the arrival of this mutual openness and unreserve.'

The literature definitions of therapeutic touch vary from a simple hand contact to a full embrace, but it is important to stress that consistent in all definitions is the clear statement that responsible therapeutic touch is non-erotic. For example, touch has been defined by Bacorn and Dixon (1984) as 'physi-cal contact between the hands of the counsellor and the hands, arms, shoulders, legs or upper back of the client.' They stress that the areas of a subject's body permissible to touch were chosen to guarantee that the touch recipient interpret the touch as warm, friendly and pleasant rather than aggressive, exploitative or sexual in intent.

Suiter and Goodyear (1985) in their study used three levels

of touch: touch of the client's hand, touch of the client's shoulder, and semi-embrace. Casher (1967), Mintz (1969) and Robertiello (1974) all consider touch to be an important communication technique but issue the warning that it must be carefully considered before being employed. Forer (1969) saw value in the therapist touching the patient, and felt that 'guiltless contact with others is reassuring that one is a bounded person but not alone. Verbal contact alone leaves one in a limbo of isolation from one's own body and from other persons'. He also contends that touching makes for mutuality and is part of the process of testing whether one dares to become or will be permitted to become an equal. Forer, however, issues a warning note: 'Skin contact is potent stuff, precious and also dangerous. It can speed up or restimulate therapy that is bogged down in trivial verbal details. But to use it casually without much talk and exploration, without conscious assessment of its impact and relevance, is foolish.'

While a number of psychotherapists have written in support of touch others have expressed concern that touching may interfere with transference, foster dependency and be detrimental to the therapeutic relationship. Jones (1955) and Wolberg (1967) both submit that therapy has effectively stopped once physical contact is introduced. Stockwell and Dye (1980) studied the effect of counsellor touch on clients' evaluation of counselling and level of self-exploration, and found that it did not have a significant outcome. Their experiment complicates the debate over the use of touch in counselling and indicates that further research is necessary.

Such research on touch in counselling to date has been mixed, with none of the studies showing results in a consistent direction. Mintz (1969) pointed out that 'it is a source of recurrent amazement – that the dimension of physical contact between therapist and patient has been almost ignored in the literature of psychotherapy.'

There appear to be three general schools of thought on the use of touch. The first strongly advocates its use; the second is strongly opposed, while the third school indicates that the use of touch may be valuable when the counsellor is aware of the patient's dynamics and of the possible interpretations of the touch gesture. In a study of the effects of touch on depressed and vocationally undecided clients, Bacorn and

Dixon (1984) attempted to assess the effects of tactile contact on the clients' perceptions of the counsellor and the counselling relationship. Every subject in the 'touch conditions' was touched four times by means of (a) an introductory handshake, (b) light touch on the shoulder/upper back as the subject was guided to her chair, (c) a touch on the hand, forearm, upper arm or leg during the interview, and (d) a parting handshake. Appropriate verbal language accompanied both handshakes and the touch on the shoulder or upper back. Most of the touched subjects regarded the touch as an expression of the counsellor's friendliness, warmth or caring. In many instances the word 'understanding' was used to describe the meaning that the subjects attached to the counsellor's touch. However positive most of the subjects regarded the touch, Bacorn and Dixon record that 'caveats remain in its blanket use as a counselling tool. Although touch may promote some clients' perceptions of warmth and understanding in the counsellor, it may, as some of the uncomfortable clients reported, surprise, confuse or affront others.'

There may be instances in which the counsellor's touch will interfere with the client's struggle with sensitive issues. It may also be the case that it is the counsellor's own anxiety or need for closeness that is ameliorated with the touch. There will be occasions when physical contact is misconstrued with the result that its use may simply contribute to the already considerable barriers to the client's and counsellor's mutual understanding. Touch is by no means always an instrument for increasing therapeutic effectiveness.

On the more positive side some helpful suggestions on the use and value of touch in counselling situations have been offered by Holroyd and Brodsky (1980). They advocate its usefulness with clients who present themselves as socially or emotionally immature (e.g. those with histories of maternal deprivation); with clients experiencing grief, trauma, depression or other acute distress, as a way of demonstrating general emotional support, and as a greeting or at the termination of an interview. Additional positive guidelines have been proposed by Older (1982) when practitioners wish one particular theme or message to be emphasized during an interview. He observes how 'a light touch can set the therapist's words in capital letters, can announce that this is more important than what has been said before. The touch acts as penetrating oil for the communication.' The practitioner can rest his fingers lightly on the back of the client's hand. Should the message be wounding or hurtful Older advocates that the placing of both hands around one of the client's hands may be more appropriate. Touch can help focus the attention of clients who tend to lose contact with the therapist and can serve as a 'ground control for clients who are acutely disturbed or psychotic, bringing them back to reality.' He further suggests that the power of touch is able to release repressed fear and anger, help clients talk, bring back memories and enable clients to deal with material long denied.

One who is known for her emotional involvement with patients, Fromm-Reichmann (1960), is of the opinion that:

> as to the fourth goal of human satisfaction, the avoidance of physical loneliness, it goes without saying that the patient should not be used for its achievement. This does not advocate that the psychiatrist be an obsessional denizen of our culture, wherein touching another person or being touched by him is considered taboo unless there is an intimate relationship. The contrary is true. At times it may be indicated and wise to shake hands with a patient or, in the case of a very disturbed person, to touch him reassuringly or not to refuse his gesture of seeking affection and closeness. However, it is always recommended that one be thrifty with the expression of any physical contact.

The use of physical touch in therapy as an aid to help clients achieve greater closeness in inter-personal relationships and work through their detachment and anxieties over intimacy is graphically demonstrated by Wilson (1982) in the following case-study:

> I had worked with Ms Smith in therapy for one year, her central problem being avoidance of intimacy with others. One day I touched her on the shoulder as she left the office. Two therapy sessions later, Ms Smith said to me, 'I feel so uncomfortable if someone touches me', referring to the time I touched her. She then mentioned her difficulties in her relationship with her boyfriend of six years, an area of her

life that we had not previously discussed. She had often wanted to reach out to touch him and show him affection, but had feared rejection. Within several more weeks Ms Smith was able to risk being affectionate with her boyfriend. He responded to her with surprise, but also favourably. Since the time I touched her, Ms Smith has moved farther than she had in the previous year toward breaking down her isolation from others.

Self-disclosure is a measurable facet of man's being and his behaviour. His understanding of its conditions and correlates will enrich the understanding of man in health and disease (Barnett, 1972). Patients seem to benefit from counsellors who are equally comfortable communicating in non-verbal as well as verbal modes.

Recent research findings suggest that illness begins when a person's life begins to lose zest, a sense of future, meaning and love (Jourard, 1971). Tactile contact with a patient somehow increases his sense of being a worthwhile individual person: being heard and touched by another who 'cares' seems to reinforce identity, mobilize spirit and promote self-healing. A reassuring handshake, a touch on the shoulder or arm can provide support to a client who may feel alienated from the rest of the world. Such supportive communication can serve to strengthen his body-image and bring into awareness, in a way that no words can, a sense of the body as being connected to the inner life of thoughts and feelings.

Wilson (1982) suggests that with most clients it is advisable for the therapist to refrain from using touch during the introductory phase of the relationship, when establishing trust is paramount. The one exception is 'crises' intervention. Individuals in crisis may feel overwhelmed and wish for someone to take over and care for them momentarily, as when they were small children. It becomes particularly important that they do not feel they are having to face the problem alone. To touch a client on the arm during a time of emotional trauma may help him establish a sense of hope. Touch is far more helpfully used during parts of the working-through phase of the therapeutic relationship when trust has already been established.

A common factor among depressed patients is an increased

need or wish for touch. Often they can be reached on a physical level when they fail to respond to oral communication. Physical touch can display empathy in any situation where it is difficult to express one's thoughts and feelings orally. Often the patient himself in moments of emotional turmoil or stress may reach for the hand of the therapist. In some instances it may be therapeutically beneficial for the therapist to permit this. It is important, however, for the therapist to be sufficiently aware of the patient's dynamics to understand the meaning this action may have to him or her. A mutual physical gesture may convey to some patients an acknowledgment of the therapist's knowledge and acceptance of their emotional upset, yet to others even a minimum amount of physical contact may be frightening and disturbing.

Touch has been used effectively in counselling sessions with those who have been physically or emotionally abused and with parents who abuse and neglect their children. Older (1981) suggests that if touch is the damaging modality in these instances, it may also be a source of restoration. He quotes an example of the profound effect of touch in the treatment of abusing parents where unfortunately its implications were virtually ignored:

> At a crucial time in one interview, during which Sally was crying and the worker put a sympathetic hand on her shoulder, they were interrupted by the ward personnel demanding Sally come out and join in the routine group therapy scheduled at that time. She later described the situation as follows: 'When Mrs D. put her hand on my shoulder, I felt a sense of hope for the first time in my life, and then they ruined the whole thing.' (Steele and Pollack, 1974)

This theory is further endorsed by Wilson (1982) who has used touch effectively with parents who physically and emotionally neglect and abuse their offspring. Using touch in therapy can provide a model of the response that adequate and loving parents give their child. This is illustrated in the following case-study:

Mrs Roberts was referred to me after deliberately burning

her eight-year old son's fingers on the stove. When Mrs Roberts finally arrived for the appointment, after I had made several telephone attempts to engage her, she appeared disorganized, angry and defensive. She gave an elaborate, pressured explanation, blaming the older son for making her angry enough to burn her younger son's fingers. The more verbal interventions I made, the less she talked about her feelings and responsibility in the incident. Since she responded to my verbal questioning with such guardedness I stopped, took her hands in mine, and reflected to her that she was feeling much pressure and was carrying a heavy burden. Her eyes filled with tears, she squeezed my hands and nodded her head in agreement. Her harsh affect changed into a sad soft one. She had verbalized her fear of losing control and seriously hurting her son. At the end of the interview. Mrs Roberts made future plans with me to continue therapy. I walked her out of my office with my arm around her shoulder. She has subsequently continued therapy for several months. Although it has been a struggle, with support and re-learning experience including touching, Mrs Roberts had maintained control in caring for her son.

There also appear to be three distinct schools of thought in psychiatric nursing literature with regard to touch in patient care. Generally nurses describe touch favourably, yet as one allows for individual differences in a patient's perception of touch, so too one must allow for the individual differences of approach and attitude in those of a nurse. Some nurses may vary in the degree of comfort they themselves experience as the initiator and recipient of touch (Johnson, 1965). Others may feel that by touching patients they are becoming over-involved with their patients or vulnerable to their demands (Mercer, 1966). A patient may need to touch and be touched by the nurse to reassure him that the nurse is a 'real' person. The nurse should be sensitive enough to be aware when closeness is acceptable and when it is not; she must determine how the patient might interpret and respond to it. In a study with psychiatric nurses Aquilera (1967) found that they could elicit more verbal interaction from patients they touched than when they were not touched.

There should be a sensitive interplay of feeling between nurse and patient. Physical touch can be a most effective channel of non-verbal communication but it has to be 'appropriately timed, in the appropriate context, with the appropriate individual' (Farrah, 1971). This means that the nurse has to be aware of its potentialities as well as its limitations. Some of the hazards involved in using touch in the psychiatric setting have been commented upon by de Augustinis et al. (1963). They estimated in their study that the nurses' use of touch may have been misinterpreted by patients as much as 50 per cent of the time.

To the pyscho-geriatric patient, often confused and disorientated, withdrawn and depressed, a sense of being touched can be something very special. It can help break down isolation – sensory, social, emotional and physiological. A medical officer working in a psychiatric hospital records a visit paid to his hospital by an Anglican bishop.

> In the dayroom of the psycho-geriatric ward, which houses the most dependent patients, he [the bishop] declared himself much impressed by the performance of the percussion band, played by the patients with some assistance from stereo and staff. When the music stopped, I whispered in his ear, 'They would be thrilled if you shook hands with them.' The bishop did so – with them all. The next morning, an 85 year old still with some command of words said, 'Do you know, doctor, he shook hands with each one of us. It was like a personal blessing.' (Henley, 1977)

The need to touch and be touched is often found to be prevalent in schizophrenic patients and some who suffer from neurotic tendencies. By definition 'schizophrenia' is regression to the primary process, and to a primary narcissism. The patient is subconsciously seeking human relatedness. Whether such expectations can and should be met is a most complex issue. (Hannah Green's novel *I Never Promised You a Rose-Garden*, Pan Books 1967, portrays a most vivid account of 'the dark kingdom of the mind' of a young schizophrenic patient.) 'Offering one's hand to a patient . . . can have overtones which might appear to be undesirable in treatment or it can on the simplest level be a reinforcement of the encounter' (Burton and Heller, 1964).

Often regressed schizophrenic patients stretch out their hands to touch in a substituted form of communication and to reassure themselves of their continuity and existence. One of the major obstacles in the psychotherapy of schizophrenic patients is their characteristic lack of readiness to accept the therapist as a working partner in a personal relationship. The schizophrenic appears to be motivated by a fearful and hateful lack of faith in himself and others.

In a study of schizophrenic patients Lowen (1969) showed how the failure of early tactile contact is related to this mental disorder. Pleasurable body contact between mother and child appears to have been absent. He observed how the feeling of identity arises from a feeling of body contact. 'To know who he is, the person must be aware of what he feels. In the schizophrenic patient this is precisely what appears to be lacking: he is out of touch with reality. His conscious sense of identity is unrelated to the world and to people.' Lack of physical intimacy has resulted in feelings of abandonment. Sechehaye (1951) describes how she made herself understood to a young schizophrenic girl by means of symbolic signs, gestures and movements, especially when she put her arm around the patient's shoulders.

Montagu (1971) notes that the extraordinary frequency with which one comes upon accounts of 'break-throughs' brought about by bodily contact in reaching schizophrenics, who had for years been inaccessible to other therapeutic approaches, is striking. In discussing the use of touch with such patients Robertiello (1974), assuming that a major focus of the therapy involved therapist and client recreating the relationship between mother and child during the first year of life, held patients when they expressed feelings of wanting to be held. He found such physical contact of value in helping patients work through their detachment and anxieties over intimacy, and in attaining greater closeness in relationships outside therapy.

Extra holding has been reported to enhance the intellectual development of retarded infants who are confined to institutions. Various researchers have observed that tactile experiences play an important role in the therapy of severely disturbed children. Often their body language symbolizes that words are often meaningless: it is a dialogue of touch for which they long. They yearn not for a mere token interest that will momentarily satisfy a need, but for a 'depth-penetrating Chardinian "hominisation" to fill their deep void' (Hoffman, 1967). When a finger touches or a hand is clasped or when an arm is placed around a shoulder an emotionally disturbed child can be assured: 'I accept you as you are; accept me as I am, because you and I can be one with the bond of together-ness.' In a study by Norberg (1986) with two patients in the final stage of dementia it was observed how they were stimulated with music and touch. It is a challenging task to find means to communicate as efficiently as possible with such patients. The study revealed that brain-damaged patients can retain their ability to react to touch when they do not react to verbal conversation, as 'the earliest and most elementary medium of human communication is the art of touch' (Barnett, 1972). One patient who had been diagnosed as having organic brain disease remarked to the leader of a group session, 'You are my relative.' When questioned about such a statement, he replied, 'You touched me, therefore we are related.'

The former Bishop of Peru recalls:

> taking the Bishop of Bethlehem from a church in the United States to visit patients in the Mother Theresa Home in Lima, Peru. We were talking to a person of indeterminate age; perhaps in the young 30s. He was sitting in a type of high-chair. He had no legs from the knee downwards and his arms were distorted. He was unable to speak properly and was making inarticulate sounds. I remember vividly trying to say something to him and feeling that nothing I said communicated with him. The Bishop of Bethlehem, who was with me, started gently to stroke the stump of the leg of this patient. The effect on the patient was electric. He calmed down immediately, his arms ceased to gesticulate and his eyes sought to focus on the person responsible for touching him. He was a vivid lesson of the reality of the personal communication through touch that was so much stronger than words. (Evans, 1988)

Many of the mentally and physically handicapped, some of whom have spent almost a life-time in institutions, have been deprived of touch. Those who have been so deprived because

they have lived a life of brokenness and abandonment cry out
for touch – a touch which confirms their 'loveableness', gives
them a sense of belonging and grants them a certain inner
peace. Being touched symbolizes for them, 'I exist and I am
worthy of care.' It is a closed world in which they live and
they struggle to get out. They struggle to make contact with
their environment and with the persons in it. They reach out
in the only way they know how. They are eager to shake
hands, to touch, to communicate. In ministering to them it
is also important that we too search for what in them makes
us want to back off and withdraw. We have to be honest
about the feelings the mentally and physically handicapped
create in us and where they make us anxious. We often
withdraw because communication with them demands a great
deal of our personhood and there is the possibility that 'we
will be found to be stupid and insignificant' (Stubblefield,
1970).

Even if they have not been deprived of touch in younger
days they manifest their need of physical contact in ways
which many other people would not dare. In their manifestations they are far more natural than so called 'normal'
people.

In our Western world, as we have already noted, touch has
become very much 'sexualized', and consequently appears to
be dangerous. Every human being needs touch and needs to
give touch as a mode of true, simple and loving expression:
it is a mode of demonstrating affection and concern for other
people. For those who are handicapped it is more 'permissible': it is seen as a cry for identity, an urge for communication and acceptance.

'It is a wonderful thing', states Vanier (1973),

> when you put your arms out in a welcoming attitude to a
> handicapped person; then something happens: his eyes
> begin to believe and his heart begins to dance and he begins
> in some way to become our teacher . . . we can teach little
> but we are taught a lot . . . I begin to discover something:
> that this wounded person looks at me, approaches me – all
> this does something to me, the wounded person calls me
> forth . . . we are brought to life by the eyes and hands and
> call of wounded people who seem to call us forth to life.

101

As soon as we touch a severely handicapped person with love we enter into contact and we discover that he is truly a human being: the real person is revealed no matter how ravaged or distorted the mind or body might be, and we and our brother or sister become one.

The mentally handicapped cannot fully understand the finer concepts of words or of language and so physical contact becomes one of their major instruments of communication. By touch they can unmask our irritations and lack of interest. With outstretched hands they seek for true friendship and genuine relationship, and are often able to sense the difference between the possessive, patronizing touch and the genuine, supportive and related touch. The following comment of one who was caring for a multi-handicapped child illustrates this graphically. 'When I am irritated or angry I can hide this in my voice and even in the way I look at S. but she obviously feels it in the way I handle her, even if I try very hard not to show it. . . . She always screams when I am angry or irritated. . . . She is a tremendous challenge to me.' In all the warmth and security of physical intimacy there must still remain a distance so that the uniqueness of each individual is preserved. The utmost discretion is needed to know how close we can become to whom.

Massage can have surprisingly powerful effects on mental, physical and even emotional health, and is being used in various centres which care for the mentally and physically handicapped. Tension is often relieved and dissolves into relaxed pleasure and calm. Often it is accompanied by meditative relaxation music. For many of the handicapped it can become their most sensory experience. Such personal attention of a relaxed sympathetic approach inevitably benefits them greatly.

Touch is one of the several ways of communication that our Western world has 'misplaced', and which people who are marginalized by society are helping us to rediscover (T. Vanier, 1988). 'Handicapped people are very vulnerable', writes Nouwen (1986),

but this vulnerability also allows them to bear ample fruit in the lives of those who receive them. They are grateful people. They know they are dependent on others and show this dependence every moment; but their smiles, embraces, kisses are offered as spontaneous expressions of thanks. . . . They do not read newspapers, watch TV, or discuss the possibility of a future disaster. They do not dwell upon the future. Instead they say: 'Feed me, dress me, touch me, hold me, kiss me, speak to me.'

In considering the use of touch in counselling and psychotherapy it is wise to bear in mind that there are unique dangers and disadvantages in applying it as a therapeutic measure. As a result of intra-psychic difficulties or past experiences the patient may be led to interpret the therapist's well-intentioned gesture as a sexual advance. It is Marmer (1976) who notes that '. . . most erotic breaches of the therapist-patient relationship occur with women who are physically attractive, almost never with the aged, the infirm or the ugly!' Far more serious problems arise when the therapist's personal insecurity may lead to loss of control and touching gestures go beyond the bounds of the therapeutic. The professional therapist must always have a clear understanding of what is transpiring in therapy.

There will be instances when it is inadvisable to use touch in therapy, and Older (1982) suggests avoiding its use if the counsellor or therapist (a) does not want to touch the client; (b) senses that the client does not want to be touched; (c) wishes to touch and senses that the client wishes to be touched, but does not believe touch would be effective; (d) feels manipulated, conned or coerced into touching, or (e) is aware of feelings of manipulating or coercing the client through touch. He also lists certain categories of clients for whom touch seems inadvisable: 'Touch a paranoid and risk losing a tooth; touch a seductress and risk losing your licence, touch a violent patient with a short fuse and risk losing everything!'

Appropriate touch becomes inappropriate when given at the wrong time, in the wrong dose or to the wrong person. On the other hand it has been shown how avoidance of tactile contact by the therapist may recreate the experience of physical rejection, and also reinforce the denial of bodily awareness, particularly with obsessional and schizoid personalities (Mintz, 1969). The counsellor should always be aware of the potential power implications of physical touch and clear about his own attitude towards its use in therapy. He should not only know himself but also his clients. He needs, too, to be aware of his own countertransference feelings.

As there is no formula for touching in counselling and psychotherapy a professional judgement about the appropriateness of its use should be made in each situation. The therapist has to judge whether his own use of touch will contribute to the further wellbeing and mental health of his clients.

Some words of Carl Rogers (1961) sum up the therapeutic situation admirably:

> I started from a thoroughly objective point of view. Psychotherapeutic treatment involved the diagnosis and analysis of the client's difficulties, the cautious interpretation and explanation to the client of the causes of his difficulties and a re-educative process focused by the clinician upon the specific causal elements. Gradually I observed that I was more effective if I could create a psychological climate in which the client could undertake these functions himself – exploring, analysing, understanding and trying new solutions to his problems. During more recent years, I have been forced to recognize that the most important ingredient in creating this climate is that it should be *real*. I have come to realize that only when I am able to be a transparently real person, and am so perceived by my client, can he discover what is real in him. Then my empathy and acceptance can be effective. When I fall short in therapy, it is when I am unable to be what I deeply am. The essence of therapy, as I see it carried on by myself and others, is a meeting of two *persons* in which the therapist is openly and freely himself and evidences this perhaps more fully when he can freely and acceptantly enter into the world of the other.

Aquilera, D.   'The relationship between physical contact and verbal interaction between nurses and patients', *J. Psychiat. Nursing*, 5 (1967), pp. 5–21.

Bacorn, C. N., and Dixon, D. N.
'The effects of touch on depressed and vocationally undecided clients', *J. Couns. Psychology*, 31:4 (1984), pp. 488–496.

Barnett, K.
'A survey of the current utilization of touch by health team personnel with hospitalized patients', *Int. J. Nurs. Studies*, 9 (1972), pp. 195–209.

Burton, A., and Heller, L. G.
'The touching of the body', *Psychoanal. Review*, 51 (1964), pp. 122–134.

Cashar, L., and Dixon, B. K.
'The therapeutic use of touch', *J. Psychiatric Nursing*, 5 (1967), pp. 442–451.

Cohen, J.
Quoted in *Personality Dynamics*. Rand McNally 1969.

de Augustinis, J.
'Ward study. The meaning of touch in inter-personal communication', in *Some Clinical Approaches to Psychiatric Nursing*, eds S. F. Burd and M. A. Marshall. The Macmillan Co. 1963, pp. 271–306.

Erikson, E. H.
'Identity and the life-cycle. Selected papers', *Psychol. Issues*, 1 (1959), pp. 1–171.

Evans, D.
Personal communication (1988).

Forer, B. R.
'The taboo against touching in psychotherapy', *Psychother. Theory, Research and Practice*, 6:4 (1969), pp. 229–231.

Freud, S., and Breuer, J.
Studies in Hysteria (1893–1895). Basic Books, New York 1957.

Fromm-Reichmann, F.
Principles of Intensive Psychotherapy. Univ. of Chicago Press (Phoenix Edition) Chicago 1960.

Henley, W. E.
'A touch of the hand', *N.Z. Med. J.*, 86 (1977), pp. 100–102.

Hoffman, A.
'A dialogue of touch', *Mental Hygiene*, 5 (1967), p. 24.

Holroyd, J., and Brodsky, A.
'Does touching patients lead to sexual intercourse?' *Professional Psychology*, 11 (1980), pp. 807–811.

Johnson, B. S.
'The meaning of touch in nursing', *Nursing Outlook*, 13 (1965), pp. 59–60.

Jones, E.
The Life and Works of Sigmund Freud. 1955

	(Letter from Freud to Ferenczi, 13 Dec. 1931).
Jourard, S. M.	*Disclosing Man to Himself.* Van Nostrand, Princetown, New Jersey 1968.
Lowen, A.	*The Language of the Body.* Collier Books, New York 1971.
Marmer, J.	'Some psychodynamic aspects of the seduction of patients in psychotherapy', *Amer. J. Psychoanal.*, 36 (1976), pp. 319–323.
Menninger, K.	*Theory of Psychoanalytic Technique.* Basic Books, New York 1958.
Mercer, L. S.	'Touch: comfort or threat', *Perspectives in Psychiatric Care*, 4 (1966), pp. 20–25.
Mintz, E.	'On the rationale of touch in psychotherapy', *Psychother. Theory, Research and Practice*, 6:4 (1969), pp. 232–234.
Montagu, A.	*Touching: The Human Significance of the Skin.* Columbia Univ. Press, New York 1971.
Norberg, A., et al.	'Reactions to music, touch and object presentation in the final stage of dementia: an exploratory study', *Int. J. Nursing Stud.*, 23 (1986), pp. 315–323.
Nouwen, H.	*Life Signs: Intimacy, Fecundity and Ecstasy in Christian Perspective.* Doubleday & Co. Inc., New York 1986.
Older, J.	*Touching is Healing.* Stein & Day Publ., New York 1982.
	'Four taboos that may limit the success of psychotherapy', *Psychiatry*, 40 (1977), pp. 197–204.
Pattison, J. E.	'Effects of touch on self-exploration and the therapeutic relationship', *J. Counselling & Clinical Psychology*, 40 (1973), pp. 170–175.
Robertiello, R.	'Addendum to object relations technique', *Psychother. Theory, Research and Practice*, 11 (1974), pp. 197–204.
Rogers, C.	'Two divergent trends', in *Existential Psychology* ed. R. May. Random House, New York 1961, p. 88.
	Quoted in A. Burton and L. G Heller, 'The touching of the body', *Psychoanal. Review*, 51 (1964), pp. 122–134.

Sechehaye, M.   *Symbolic Realization*. Inter. Universities Press, New York 1951.

Spiegel, R.   'Specific problems of communication', in *American Handbook on Psychiatry*, ed. S. Arieti. Basic Books, New York 1959.

Steele, B., and   'A psychiatric study of parents who abuse
Pollack, C. B.   infants and children', in *The Battered Child* (2nd ed.), eds R. Helfer and C. H. Kempe. University of Chicago Press, Chicago 1974. Quoted in 'A restoring touch for abusing families', J. Older, *Child Abuse & Neglect*, 5 (1981), pp. 487–489.

Stockwell, S. R., and   'Effects of counsellor touch on counselling
Dye, A.   outcome', *J. Couns. Psychology*, 27:5 (1980), pp. 443–446.

Stubblefield, H. W.   'On being a pastor to the mentally retarded', *J. Past. Care.*, XXIV (1970), pp. 98–108.

Suiter, R. L., and   'Male and female counsellor and client
Goodyear, R. K.   perceptions of four levels of counsellor touch', *J. Couns. Psychology*, 32:4 (1985), pp. 645–648.

Vanier, J.   *Tears of Silence*. Darton Longman & Todd, London 1976.

Vanier, T.   Personal communication (1988).

Wilson, J. M.   'The value of touch in psychotherapy', *Amer. J. Orthopsychiat.*, 52 (1982), pp. 65–72.

Wolberg, L.   *The Technique of Psychotherapy*. Grune and Stratton, New York 1958.

6

Touch in the Care of the Aged, Dying and Bereaved

But O! For the touch of a vanish'd hand
And the sound of a voice that is still.

Tennyson, 'Break, break, break'

THE AGED

The need for touch does not appear to increase or decrease with age. Montagu (1971) believed that in the aged the hunger for tactile stimulation often remains unsatisfied and leads to disappointment and failure to communicate. In studying the perception of touch in the elderly, physiological and behavioural changes have to be taken into account as part of the aging process. Factors such as sensory impairment, multiple illnesses, disorientation and attitudes toward aging magnify sensory and perceptual deficits in other systems. Such disabilities, compounded by the lack of meaningful touch with others, make the isolation of the aged even more acute.

Many of the elderly have lost their parents and spouse, and in some instances children, with whom they had exchanged a loving type of touching. In old age they seem to have no one to touch or be touched by. Grandparents generally enjoy touching their grandchildren to express their affection for them. Some very young grandchildren may be inclined to reject their grandparent's touch because, 'grandma is old, frail, wrinkled and her skin is thin and rough.'

Tobiason (1981) records that when her family visits her mother she has noticed that most of her interaction with her two children, aged five and eight years, involves touch. The children either sit on her lap or sit so close to her that their bodies touch as she reads to them. 'As we bid her farewell with kisses and hugs, she reminds us "that is what I miss most since your Dad died".' Touch and closeness all help in compensating for the loss of loved ones.

Loss of gratification in work and in an active social life in the group combine to give the aged person a deep sense of helplessness. In turn this may cause a heightened need to depend upon others in a life situation in which relationships are less sustaining than before. It has been noted that a number of lonely older women go to their hairdresser more frequently so that they can be touched by another human being. They have a wish to feel adequate, long to be needed at a time when reality makes their wishes unrealistic, and they strive for a feeling of safety and security.

The lowered self-esteem and change of body image in many of the elderly help to instil in them a feeling that in some way they are 'untouchable'. The warm welcoming hand of the carer can help to restore a sense of self-esteem. The greater the feeling of depersonalization the greater the need for identity through touch. In the care of disturbed elderly people the sense of touch is special; isolation is decreased, interaction strengthened and the presence and availability of the care-giver is established. Touching symbolizes caring and is a validation of one's existence. Some elderly folk respond to non-verbal communication when other forms bring no response. A simple gesture such as touching an elderly regressed person often does more to help than sophisticated techniques (Burnside, 1973). The need of the confused elderly to touch is greater than the need to verbalize, and offers reinforcement on a level more coincident with deficit status.

Little research has been carried out on the effect of touch on communication with the elderly who are permanently in care. Greenberg (1972) noted a trend toward improvement in psychotic behaviour in ten institutionalized elderly patients when they were touched at regular intervals during the day. One study (Burnside, 1973) reports a subjective improvement in responses when touch was used with a group of six regressed patients with chronic brain syndrome. By using touch as the primary intervention Burnside increased appropriate verbal communication and eye contact. She shook each patient's hand at the beginning and end of each group meeting. Frequently she placed her hand on the person's shoulder when speaking to him. One member of the group,

> Mrs E. who kept her eyes closed most of the time, opens them now when I touch her . . . much of her fidgeting has ceased and she seems a more relaxed little lady whose eyes are open more of the time. She said a distinct 'no' recently instead of babbling at me. She also likes to touch my clothing. I wear wild, bright-coloured clothing on group day, often with the tactile quality of cashmere or velveteen. Touching, of course, is a two-way affair – I touch them and I let them touch me, my clothing, and my jewellery. . . . They continue to teach me much about human behaviour, including my own.

The elderly cling to their possessions that can be handled or that evoke memories of lost contact. Their need for physical contact is greater because of their decreased visual, hearing and functional capabilities (Hollinger, 1980).

Burnside also points out that much can be learned from grasping an elderly person's hand, such as warmth, clamminess, perspiration, arthritis and very thin hands. Does the person cling or want to release her hand immediately? The response may provide clues about the elderly person's degree of dependence and need for touch. She cautions that one should never pat the head of an elderly person who is seated in a wheelchair, for such a gesture, frequently used in dealing with young children, can be seen as patronizing.

A study by de Wever (1977) dealing with nursing-home patients' perception of nurses' affective touching, found that putting an arm around a patient's shoulders was the touching behaviour perceived as uncomfortable by the greatest number of patients. A nurse placing his/her hand on a patient's arm was the touching behaviour perceived as most comfortable. The physical barriers in the institutionalized setting (cotsides, geriatric chairs, wheelchairs) tend to decrease sensory input. Beds with rail-sides tend to wall off the elderly patient from physical contact with others.

Touch is one means to stimulate and involve older people with themselves and with other people. They rely upon touch to gather information about the environment. In a survey undertaken by Barnett (1972) with health personnel and

110

patients in two general hospitals it was found that the age group with the most infrequent touches was the 66 to 100 year old group. The data suggest that old people are not often touched in our society. Just as children use touch as a dominant means of communication, so elderly people resort to touch to substitute for incomplete messages received through failing sensory channels. An empathetic physical touch assures the elderly that they are in safe hands. For the agitated, confused and regressed patients the need is especially clear. As the external self changes and diminishes as a result of aging or illness, the internal self-image can be nurtured and strengthened by physical touch. Such tactile contact offered with care, compassion and acceptance sustains the growth and development of their internal self-image. It helps them to feel more alive and in deeper contact with the world about them. It reaches through their loneliness and isolation and expresses love, affection and warmth. Sadly the elderly can become the untouched, the forgotten.

'It's actually the old who suffer most in our society. They are touched perhaps less than anyone – in fact, it sometimes seems as if people are afraid old age might be contagious – and this literal loss of contact must add greatly to the old person's sense of isolation' (Davis, 1972).

The carer's role with the elderly has been well described by Jourard (1971) as an 'inspiring' one, providing a sense of worth, hope and purpose in existence. By means of the caregiver's presence, touch and attempts to understand the feelings and fears of the elderly, the message is transmitted that the patient is worthy and accepted.

Feelings of isolation and loneliness can lead to a desire to retreat from all interactions and social activities. This can be exacerbated if old age itself decreases mobility and independence. Powerlessness in the elderly is a pervasive feeling that undermines the person's sense of self, self-efficiency and decision-making abilities. Tactile gestures can serve as 'illustrators' (Ekman and Friesen, 1972) augmenting speech and facilitating communication when speech becomes difficult or awkward.

THE DYING

In ministering to the dying patient cure assumes less importance, while care and relationship become paramount. The
touch of person to person in an atmosphere of love and
compassion reveals how 'holding a hand, or wiping a brow
can be as meaningful as prayer and, if spontaneous, frequently
more helpful. The sheer physical weakness and weariness of
dying makes possible a profound sacramental significance in
the most ordinary actions' (Cope, 1970). The presence of one
who can talk calmly and unemotionally about death, who
can listen quietly and convey understanding, who can sit
prayerfully in the companionship that goes beyond words,
speaks more loudly about life and love than any words spoken
no matter how affectionately or eloquently. The more intimate
the relationship has become, the more important it is that
the contacts be more frequent. Death is met best when the
dying person senses that he is accepted and understood as he
is, and that he is not alone as he faces the end of his human
existence.

Physical contact can become a 'language of relationships'
– a language which allows the carer to communicate a healing
message to those who may be struggling in doubt, loneliness
and fear. It is far from easy to relate to the depths of another
person. To do so is to come alive to his personhood, to his
pain and potential, his emptiness or fullness, his own unique
blend of hope and despair. It is painful to relate to the depths
of another, above all the dying, because it inevitably exposes
us to the dark rooms of our own inner world. His emptiness
reminds us of our own: his dying recalls our own finiteness
and fragility: his anger and guilt cause ours to resonate. Yet
only as we relate to the dying in depth can we become
'growth-facilitators' in their lives.

Holding the hand of a dying patient while talking to her
or even placing an arm around her shoulder conveys a positive
message: 'No matter what happens I shall be with you – I
won't let you down.' It means that the carer is not going to
keep his distance at all costs: the patient is being met at her
own personal level. She is being accepted as she is. 'In these
days', writes Taylor (1972), 'more and more people are sick
and lost because they do not know with any certainty who

112

they are and what they are. They can find their identity and role only when someone else sees them with love . . . no one can change or give himself until he has a self to give.'

The terminally ill often feel the need of tangible contact with those who are ministering to them: physical touch gives a physical expression to the personal relationship. Sitting at the bedside holding a hand in silence can be immensely supportive, as illustrated in the following account by a nurse:

> I was walking down the corridor . . . about seven-thirty one morning when I heard two nurses talking about their concern for one of our patients, Mr R.; I offered to help. We stepped into the room he shared with two other men and I saw that Mr R.'s breathing was deep and laboured. A nurse turned the oxygen higher . . . I was asked to stay with him. Feeling a little confused I held out my hand to him, saying softly, 'Take my hand'. His grip was very strong and I had the feeling that he was afraid. I spoke his name again and there was a response, a faint murmur. 'I'll stay here with him', I said. 'Please try to relax' . . . while he was still holding my right hand . . . his breathing was becoming heavy again . . . his lips looked dry, parched . . . his eyes had closed, but his grip was still strong on my hand . . . alone with him, it was absolutely still except for his breathing and a cough now and then . . . he still held my hand but I found myself breathing with him . . . and then he stopped breathing and his grip slipped away. . . . It had been only a little while – or perhaps a long hour – to my patient. But he did know someone was with him, just to hold his hand. I am thankful that in those last moments I could be a little comfort to him. (Hurtt, 1982)

The fear of dying is a matter distinct from the anticipation of death. The fear of death, of which many patients speak, is in fact a specific attitude toward the process of dying, and is not related to death (Weissman and Hackett, 1961). Terminal illness often creates a deep sense of disintegration with its accompanying anxiety and insecurity, and physical contact can be of much support. It is an outward and tangible sign of an inner and ready acceptance. As one patient expresses it: 'I remember very little of what was happening about me, but the two things which seemed to give me reassurance was

113

the voice of the chaplain and the feel of his hand in mine.' A patient in the midst of a rather distressful illness may see himself as 'abhorrent', and tactile contact does much to calm such an attitude of mind, bridging as it does the chasm between the world of the living and the world of the dying. Our summons is to assist the person to recreate a sense of significant-being for himself, whether it be existential, inspirational or transcendental – to be an individual even though he is dying (Feifel, 1963).

Non-verbal communication is as important as verbal. In all relationships the question of 'appropriate distance' arises. The physical and mental distance which governs effective and useful communication has to be constantly monitored. Some people are bad at distancing. Either they stand too close and assume an intimacy which does not exist, or they put up barriers and repel attempts to 'make contact'.

In general the person who is feeling frightened or insecure has a greater need of close physical contact with people she can trust than the person who is strong and independent. A group of hospice day-patients remarked how much they looked forward to arriving at the hospice in the morning because the staff-nurse always went out to the ambulance to greet them – 'often with a cuddle or hug and we really feel wanted and cared for.' In such circumstances physical touch can 'say so much'. We must remain close but at the same time capable of taking a detached view of what is going on (Parkes, 1978).

Intimacy enables one to share negative as well as positive experiences. A letter written by a German soldier to his wife during the last hours of the battle of Stalingrad, knowing he would not survive, concludes with the words:

> It is strange that people value things only when they are about to lose them. The vast difference is spanned by the bridge from heart to heart. . . . As long as there are shores, there will always be bridges. We should have the courage to walk on them. One bridge leads to you, the other to eternity; at the very end they are the same for me. Tomorrow I shall set forth on the last bridge. Give me your hand, so that the crossing won't be so hard.

The touch of a hand or the laying on of hands on the head

of the patient can be supportive and comforting. Although the dying person may not be able to give a sign of response to the caregiver's touch the patient may still be able to feel it and derive comfort from it. Touch also conveys an unquestioning acceptance of an often altered body-image. A former hospice member recalls:

> one patient, A., who had a cancer in the bones of his face. He had had surgery which had left a large cavity in his face. He had a prosthesis to cover and protect the cavity but seldom wore it, and as the cancer progressed, it became too small to cover the hole. A. was very much comforted by touch and liked the nurses to kiss him on his face to show they did not find him repulsive.

The dying have no place for the superficial or trivial, so all communication, whether verbal or non-verbal, must be meaningful. Effective communication may mean just staying quietly by a terminally ill patient, holding his hand or listening carefully to him. A staff member of a hospice records:

> We always endeavour to have a member of staff sit close to a dying person who is nearing the end of life. Being near to and touching conveys a willingness to watch with and be a companion 'on the way'. Although the person may be unable to give a sign of response to our touch, he may still be able to feel it and derive comfort from it.

The dying are quick to sense a warmth and real concern. In such a 'climate' they normally feel more free to talk and share their feelings. Conversation often progresses to deep and important issues as confidence is gained. Professional carers, on the whole, are essentially practical people of action who often find it difficult to 'be still', and sit, watch and listen: to absorb feelings of anger, sadness, loneliness and depression: to share the doubts and the questionnings, but never to provide glib answers or deceitful reassurances. 'We are not taught to hold their hands when they [i.e. the dying] are lonely or afraid, or to cradle them sobbing in our arms, smoothing the hair, holding them until the paroxysms pass', states a physician in a hospice for the terminally ill.

We are not trained to love. Or rather we are trained to

suppress our love, to don a protective uniform especially
for work: a uniform that keeps us at a safe distance from
our patients so that our meetings are those of professional
and client, not of the frail human beings that we are all.
(Cassidy, 1988)

The importance of eye-contact, physical proximity and a
friendly reassuring tone of voice cannot be over-emphasized.
Persons who are terminally ill lose a sense of worth if they
are left alone, if they are avoided and not touched or if they
receive only bland pleasantness. Communication with the
dying patient is not limited to words. Many times words are
insufficient and ineffective, meaningless and cold.

The feelings of isolation and the need for identity and
companionship are well described in the words of a patient
in his late 40s suffering from leukemia:

I wish I could tell them somehow just what it was like to
be in isolation. My wife and my family couldn't come near
me – they had to stand at the door with masks on. The
only one who was allowed to touch me was a nurse, who
had been specially cleared as being in good health (patients
undergoing chemotherapy are highly susceptible to infection, and even a common cold is potentially lethal!). This
nurse changed my bedding and kept me clean and all that.
But she hated to touch me, or at least, it felt that way.
Whatever she was doing she did with as little physical
contact as possible.

I wish I could have told them how important touch was.
I craved the feeling of flesh on flesh. I craved it! It wasn't
a sexual thing – in my condition it was the last thing on
my mind – but I really felt I was losing my will to live
without that touch. I mean I still wanted to live, to get
better, but the reason to keep struggling was slipping away
from me. I needed the feeling of someone's skin on mine
to help me find it again. (Older, 1982)

Those who tend the dying need to guard against merely
going through procedures in place of being personally
involved. Touching and physical contact are as essential as
taking care of their emotional and spiritual needs (Kubler-
Ross, 1971, 1988). '. . . At the very end, he [the dying patient]

116

will want only one loved person . . . someone who can sit silently and comfortably by his side, without words, but just touching his hand or perhaps stroking his hair or just being there.' Once the dying are deprived of communication they cannot maintain identity and role. A caring touch demonstrates empathy and is one way of 'giving permission' to patients and relatives to reveal their anxieties and distress. However, it also has its problems for timing is so essential. If used too early it can 'switch off' the expression of feelings, especially if accompanied by such expressions as, 'don't cry', 'don't upset yourself!'

Touch can be an important part of caring for the dying but as with every aspect of care the needs of both patients and family members must be assessed. There will be situations where physical contact, a touch on the hand of the patient or relative, is reassuring, but the degree of contact offered requires sensitivity. While there are many occasions when a comforting arm around a shoulder is appropriate, for some this will be an unwanted intrusion. There are times when privacy will be needed. Touch may even be contraindicated for certain individuals or in certain circumstances. Unlike verbal communication, the message conveyed by means of touch cannot be easily changed or corrected. It is therefore important not only to consider each patient individually but also to have an accurate perception of how patients interpret the touch. We ourselves have to be aware of our own responses to touching patients. By being authentic we can communicate our real intent.

The relationship previously established will indicate how touch should be handled (Lichter, 1987). One can pick up cues about its relevance from body language. It can be extremely helpful at the end of a first visit to bid farewell with a light touch on the arm or hand. The reaction to this may help indicate whether touch will be an appropriate part of care or not.

The carer has to feel comfortable about the act of touch to use it effectively in ministering to the dying. To feel uncomfortable is sometimes a warning sign against using it in a particular situation. Absence of touch can also be significant. One patient in a hospice remarked: 'The doctor stops examining you when you're terminally ill.' Visitors, including relatives, often withdraw from the bedside and so leave the patient not only mentally and emotionally but physically isolated as well. 'The kiss on the lips becomes a peck on the forehead, then the light touch on the arm, then the wave from the door. When the doctor visits, he stands at the foot of the bed' (Lichter, 1984).

Warmth rather than authority reassures the patient. A university professor writing on his own dying, described how the actions of hospital personnel made him feel like an 'object'. His illness seemed:

> to demonstrate to people that I'm not really people any more, I'm somebody else. I'm a body that has some very interesting characteristics about it, which include twitching of the muscles, rather symptomatic of this particular disease . . . I felt treated as an object! Being a patient is one thing, but being an object is even less than being a patient!

The combination of separation and objectivity helps to create the feeling of depersonalization – a state of 'non-being'. The terminally ill look to non-verbal cues for indications of acceptance and caring. Sometimes touch may be the only form of communication and expression of caring that is available, as when a patient is delirious, comatose or unconscious. The message of a caring touch may lie in its spontaneity symbolizing human feeling and companionship. 'In hospice care', recalls a hospice matron,

> we are able to practise touch, and we have time to do so. Technology has no place – the 'old-fashioned' nursing procedures are the norm. There is time to help families to hold hands, to touch, in the sharing of the sadness in which they are involved. Often, even husbands and wives have to be helped to know it is O.K. to sit holding hands. I think the circle of the family round the dying loved-one's bed – all physically in contact with one another and with, sometimes, a nurse as part of the circle, is helpful and to be encouraged . . . many of us like to use touch when praying with a patient or relation, holding the hand or placing a hand on the head.

Often fear and its manifestation can be detected in the patient who hangs on to the carer, clings to the hand, whether offered

118

or not. Gentle soothing and stroking can calm a terrified patient. Until the age of technology nursing was always predominantly a 'hands on' profession: all nursing procedures involved touching the patient to a much greater extent than they do today. Patients were confined to bed for much longer periods of time. The pace of work was slower, and time and touch went hand-in-hand.

A chaplain of a hospice relates:

> I have always held the hands of patients because I believe it helps to convey to them love and support. . . . On arriving at St A.'s one day I was met by the son of one of the female patients. He asked me to go to his mother as she was very ill. He and his brother knelt with me at her bedside and prayed. Then I put my hands on her head to bless her. In the middle of this blessing she died. A few days later I spoke to one of the sons about it, and he remarked: 'You relaxed her and helped her on her way.'

In many dying patients, the greatest threat appears not so much death, but rather the danger of progressive isolation and a sense of 'alone-ness'. One of the major roles of those who minister to them is to attempt to interpret the patient's various 'manoeuvres'; to understand how he is trying to cope with the threat, and so be able to stay with him to relieve the threat of 'abandonment'. Our own embarrassment at looking at the individual face of death forces the seriously ill and dying patient to live alone on the brink of an abyss, with no one around to understand him. One is reminded of Tolstoy's 'Ivan Ilych' where touch becomes the denouement of the whole situation. Ivan, totally isolated from all around him, cries out in despair: 'Why and for what reason, is there all this horror?' Suddenly he becomes aware of a touch of a hand – it is that of his schoolboy son. This gesture enables Ivan to die reconciled with his family. He is at peace with himself and for the first time feels love. Once we have entered into communion with the dying through touch we begin to love them much more than we could ever have loved them in life.

To stay at the bedside of the dying, to watch by them, to relate to them, to communicate with them and to learn from them without necessarily knowing all the answers to questions asked, is to symbolize our togetherness as a family.

A medical director of a hospice notes how different ways of touching can be used in the care of the terminally ill. There is the 'arm around the shoulder', signifying protection, defence against further onslaught, support at times of weakness. There is the 'held hand' symbolizing comfort and a certain intimacy of relationship. There is the 'hand gently placed on the arm' which is again warm but respectful rather than intimate, with no sexual connotation whatsoever. Finally, there is the 'patient's hand being held in both hands' of the doctor or nurse, symbolizing the complete security that they can feel in the professional carer's hands (Doyle, 1988).

There is scientific evidence that there is an important biological need of touch. This has been designated as 'skin hunger', which is also a factor in the normal development of mammals (probably all mammals, and may be other animals as well). For some patients what is required is, in the words of Patrick O'Donovan, describing his own experiences of a prolonged fatal illness, 'touch ... with just the right sort of unsentimental and affectionate respect'. Such tactile contact enables the dying to see themselves 'becoming' rather than 'diminishing'.

An important aspect of care will be to take account of and deal with the family-as-a-whole. Are they regressing? Do they understand the illness? Do they always have to be doing something? Have they already given up hope and so convey grief rather than relationship? What are some of their emotional and spiritual strengths and weaknesses? If we are to support a family through the hard times of terminal illness, it will be necessary for us to achieve a closeness which is unusual outside the family. We may need to hold a hand or put an arm round a person who is in deep distress and give them the same kind of non-verbal assurance which a mother can give to her child.

The following account demonstrates how one nurse actually helped family members touch the patient through her own example. The nurse recalls:

The man was very sick. His family was standing around, but was never very close, and I noticed that his wife and other family members never touched him. So, I started to make a point of standing close to him after I entered the room. I intentionally put my hand on his shoulder or held his hand while I talked with him. After a while, I began to see a change. His wife and the others began holding his hand and touching him in a similar manner. Their exchange was livelier, and the patient smiled more and seemed more relaxed. As they touched him more, I began touching him less.

Another nurse relates how she comforted the wife of a patient with a diagnosed malignancy of the colon. In tears the wife did not know if she could stand to watch him die. The nurse tells how

I sat down beside her and put my arm around her. I could feel her tense muscles relax. We just sat together for a while. We never again talked about her husband dying. Each time I entered the room, I put my arm around her shoulders and gave her a hug or held her hand for a few minutes. That is all she seemed to want. It seemed to me that we were talking a lot, but not out loud.

The integrity of relationship will prove far more important than any form of technique. Empathy takes preference over sympathy. Presence affords a therapy of companionship which can transform despair into hope and give light in the midst of seeming futility: it searches for the question behind the question: for the fear behind the bravado, for the insecurity behind the pretence, for the faith behind the timidity.

Touch is very much the province of the physiotherapist and it legitimizes touch in the eyes of even the most reserved of patients. Touch can be enjoyed without it appearing sentimental, or indicating some kind of unwelcome need or dependence (Lichter, 1988). A physiotherapist caring for the terminally ill states:

I do use touch a lot. The core of physiotherapy is our hands, for we are the profession which uses hands and handling to assess. I do not feel I can treat patients at arm's length, and the very nature of our work as physiotherapists is such that we must get close to our patients if we are effectively to help them with their physical rehabilitation. I can ask a patient to bend his knee while I remain just standing by his bed, or I can hold his foot and knee . . . I get far better physical response by adopting the second method. Does it not follow therefore that I shall get a better emotional response if I not only offer words of comfort, but also show my concern by stroking his hands or forehead? I can congratulate a patient on some achievement by saying 'well done', but I can communicate my pleasure more by squeezing his hand or giving him a pat on the back as well. (Chatterton, 1988)

Often during procedures that involve touch the dying patient will give vent to personal and emotional problems that are troubling him. During the bathing of a patient, particularly when the back is being washed, it appears that touch provides relaxation and assurance. It is interesting to note that the timing seems relevant when direct confrontation and eye contact are avoided. It is also one of the few occasions when both time and privacy are available. Tender loving physiotherapy, referred to by Lichter (1984) as TLP, often alleviates discomfort and is always soothing as a result of stroking, gentle massage.

Massage itself provides physical contact in a welcoming non-aggressive way, particularly where touch conveys an unquestioning acceptance of an often altered body-image. For some cancer patients, for example, months of aggressive treatments are apt to have a depersonalizing effect, sometimes to a state where they no longer recognize the self they had once known (Byass, 1988). Sims (1986) undertook a pilot study to examine the effects of gentle back massage on the perceived well-being of six female patients receiving radiotherapy for breast cancer. The patients reported less symptom distress, higher degrees of tranquillity and vitality, and less tension and tiredness. The results of massage can not only heal the body but soothe the mind and strengthen the spirit.

The need for touch seems to increase in times of stress, and many patients are receptive to touches which communicate caring and promote comfort. A staff member of a hospice writes: 'We have a beautician and some of the ladies say how therapeutic it is to be massaged, manicured and made up – all necessitating physical touch – it increases their well-being, makes them *feel* good and relaxed.' It is therefore important that where circumstances are deemed appropriate, different techniques such as massage and physiotherapy are used in such stress-related situations as described above.

THE BEREAVED

The symbol of the organization known as 'The Compassionate Friends', which helps bereaved parents, depicts two outstretched hands about to clasp each other. In bereavement when one hand reaches out and the other takes hold, they both become stronger. A sorrow shared will not necessarily alleviate grief but it reminds the bereaved that they are not alone. It is not the role of the helper to render the grief-stricken passive in their pain, nor to reassure them with premature yet well-meaning expressions of condolence, but rather to help them grieve, each in his own way and in his own time. Time must be given to absorb; time to ask questions; time to express doubts; time to go over past events; time to sit holding a hand with a friend, sharing feelings and airing them if necessary many times over. There is a tendency to want the bereaved to recover quickly, to prescribe rather than counsel and to advise rather than listen.

There is no known way of avoiding the pangs of grief. If peace is sought through evasion mourning may well be postponed indefinitely, there being intellectual recognition of the death without emotional acceptance of it. In ministering it is not ours to explain or to interpret. There are two important psychological tasks to be completed. The bereaved have to acknowledge and accept the truth that a death has actually occurred and that a bond has been broken. The bereaved then have to experience all the emotions and problems resulting from the loss, and attempt to work through them. Both take time and both are necessary requisites for recovery and eventual healing. There is 'no magical anaesthetic for the pain of grief' (Parkes, 1984). Each stage of grief has to be 'pained through' (Lindemann, 1944). Freud as well as Tolstoy compared grief with a wound that has to heal. Healing comes with the reality of mourning.

Those who mourn will inevitably have feelings of loneliness, abandonment and yearning for the lost member of family.

The most valuable offering we can give is that of our presence. Not having to grieve alone is often the most precious gift of all: 'It is far more important than our knowledge or our advice, for the companionship of family and friends is the greatest source of support and solace. We can help our grieving friend most by sitting near, holding a hand, giving a hug, listening and sharing our feelings' (Tatebaum, 1981).

Feelings of emotional distance from other people are common in bereavement and are graphically described by Lewis (1961) as 'a sort of invisible blanket between the world and me. I find it hard to take in what anyone says . . . yet I want others to be about me.' Ruth, one of the characters in Susan Hill's novel *In the Springtime of the Year* (Penguin Books 1977), widowed by the tragic fatal accident of her young husband, is comforted by her friends in her rural cottage, 'but they all seemed to be a great distance away from her, even as they filled up the small room, she heard what they said as though it came down a long tunnel.' In the initial stage of shock words often prove meaningless and the symbolic act of physical touch, a hand on a hand or arm, or around the shoulder, offers far more creative and comforting support.

To be able to stand in the right place or say all the 'right' words does not make ministry to the bereaved necessarily adequate or effective. Rule of thumb approaches are out of place. Truly to minister involves a depth of insight and understanding of the grief process. The poverty of verbal communication threatens the security of the helper, for mere expressions of sympathy, feeling sorry for people, are not enough. We have to understand as fully and sensitively as possible what this bereavement means to those who are now mourning and how best to communicate this understanding. The working through of grief has to come from within and be done by the bereaved themselves.

Newly bereaved people can usually rely on their friends and family for plenty of hugs and cuddles during the initial stage of grief, and this can afford much source of comfort. Problems arise thereafter when the number of people who feel safe to touch drops very markedly. Sometimes this results from fears of sexual involvement or 'dependency', and these fears are not always unjustified. Bereaved people easily cling to those who offer help and both may later have difficulty in undoing the attachments that result. Loss of a partner leads to much loneliness and a very conscious wish to be held. This is not always sexualized and widows in particular often make a clear distinction between their need to receive the security of a hug and the gratification of sexual needs (Parkes, 1988). Other forms of contact may be permitted. One can shake hands warmly with many bereaved persons and often lay a hand on their shoulder. Should they cry it is usual to hold out a hand and many will hold it for a while.

Different races have different taboos in caring for the bereaved. For example, in Central Brazil one tribe waits for the fact of death to be established by the cessation of breathing. They then know that the soul will not return and it is on this account that they start to weep. During the weeping the mourners crouch round the corpse and rarely stir away from it (Rosenblatt et al., 1976).

During the Maori *Tangi* which lasts for three days and two nights the family live and sleep alongside the body of the deceased – friends and relatives visit bringing gifts of food and money. They greet the dead person with each member of the family in the traditional Maori fashion, touching their nose briefly to each side of the other person's nose. Funeral rites often involve a great deal of touching both of the dead person and the bereaved family. Ritual dances are often very uninhibited and sexual taboos may be suspended. In other societies the opposite seems to happen, widows may be isolated and subjected to severe restrictions. In some tribes it is believed that the touch of a widow can be fatal! – all of which seems to reflect the mixed feelings which are involved in the grieving process.

Similarly restrictions on touching dead bodies vary greatly. Each society seems to have its own rules about who can touch and how. Often those who lay out the dead or touch them themselves become taboo and have to undergo rituals of purification. In Britain relatives may be permitted to view a dead person but they are seldom encouraged to touch the corpse. A nurse at a hospice tells how she 'always combs the dead person's hair back in front of the family and lays a hand on the shoulder, but warns them that he (or she) will feel very cold, otherwise they may get a shock if they kiss a person who has been refrigerated.'

A funeral director who specializes in dealing with those involved in disasters encourages relatives to hold any part of a body that is not badly mutilated. He instances a child whose body had been recovered from a fire. Only one hand remained normal in its appearance, but the child's mother got an immense amount of comfort from holding that hand.

Physical touch has not received much attention from most of the clinicians and researchers concerned with bereavement, yet it is acknowledged that positive feelings of sympathy, reassurance, understanding and compassion can all be transmitted by means of tactile contact. However, to be therapeutic it has to be used with the utmost discretion and sensitivity, at the right time and in the right way.

Aquilera, D. C.	'Relationship between physical contact and verbal interaction between nurses and patients', *J. Psychiat. Nurs.* (1967). pp. 15–21.
Barnett, K.	'A theoretical construct of the concepts of touch as they relate to nursing', *Nursing Research*, 21:2 (1972), pp. 102–109.
Burnside, I. M.	'Caring for the aged', *Amer. J. Nurs.*, 73 (1973), pp. 2060–2063.
Byass, R.	'Soothing body and soul', *Nursing Times*, 84 (1988), p. 24.
Cassidy, S.	*Sharing the Darkness: The Spirituality of Caring.* Darton, Longman and Todd, London 1988.
Chatterton, P.	Personal communication (1988).
Cope, G.	*Dying, Death and Disposal*, (Ed). SPCK, London 1970, p. 36.
Davis, F.	'Touching and smelling', *Glamour Mag.* (Jan 1972), p. 151.
de Wever, M. K.	'Nursing home patients' perception of nurses' affective touching', *J. Psychol.*, 96 (1977), pp. 163–171.
Doyle, D.	Personal communication (1988).
Ekman, P., and Frieson, W.	'Hand movements', *J. Commun.*, 22 (1972), pp. 353–354.
Feifel, H.	In *Taboo Topics: A Researcher's Quandary*, ed.

	N. L. Faberow. Atherton Press, New York 1963, pp. 8–21.
Greenberg, B. M.	'Therapeutic effects of touch on alteration of psychotic behavior in institutionized elderly patients' (Unpublished Master's Thesis). Duke University, USA 1972.
Hollinger, L. M.	'Perception of touch in the elderly', *J. Gerontolog. Nursing*, 6 (1980), pp. 741–746.
Hurtt, B. L.	'Take my hand', *Geriatric Nursing* (May/June 1982), pp. 1962–1964.
Jourard, S. M.	*The Transparent Self* (revised ed.). Van Nostrand Reinhold Co. 1971.
Kubler-Ross, E.	'What is it like to be dying?' *Amer. J. Nurs.*, 71 (1971), p. 1. Personal communication (1988).
Lewis, C. S.	*A Grief Observed*. Faber & Faber, London 1961.
Lichter, I.	*Communication in Cancer Care*. Churchill Livingstone, London 1987. In *Palliative Care: The Management of Far-Advanced Illness*, ed. D. Doyle. Charles Press, Philadelphia and Croom Helm, London 1984.
Lindemann, E.	'Symptomatology and management of acute grief', *Amer. J. Psychiatry*, 101 (1944), p. 147.
Montagu, A.	*Touching: The Human Significance of the Skin*. Columbia Univ. Press, New York 1971.
Older, J.	*Touching is Healing*. Stein & Day Publ., New York 1982.
Parkes, C. M.	'Psychological aspects', in *The Management of Terminal Illness*, ed. C. Saunders. Edward Arnold, London 1978. In *All in the End is Harvest*, ed. A. Whittaker. Darton, Longman & Todd in assoc. with Cruse, London 1984. Personal communication (1988).
Rosenblatt, P. C., et al.	*Grief and Mourning in Cross-Culture Perspective*. HRAF Press, Washington DC, 1976.
Seaman, L.	Quoted in 'Affective nursing touch', *Geriatr. Nurs.* (May/June 1982), pp. 162–164.
Sims, S.	'Slow stroke back massage for cancer patients', *Nursing Times*, 82:12 (1986),

	pp. 47–49.
Tatebaum, J.	*The Courage to Grieve.* Heinemann, London.
Taylor, J.	*The Go-Between God.* SCM Press, London 1972.
Tobiason, S. J. B.	'Touching is for everyone', *Amer. J. Nurs.*, 4 (1981), pp. 78–80.
Tolstoy, L.	*The Death of Ivan Ilych and Other Stories.* (Signet Classic) The New American Library 1960.
Weisman, A. D., and Hackett, T. P.	'Predilection to Death', *Psychosomatic Med.*, 23 (1961).

7

Healing Touch

At sunset all who had friends suffering from one disease or another brought them to him; and he laid his hands on them one by one. . . .

St Luke 4:40 (NEB)

It has already been noted how the use of touch in both massage and physiotherapy can be a comforting and therapeutic agent: stress can be reduced, muscular aches and pains soothed, joints unlocked and a feeling of wellbeing gained. The physician, Hippocrates, once stated that 'the physician must be experienced in many things, but assuredly in rubbing, for rubbing can bind a joint that is too loose and loosen a joint that is too rigid.' Warm baths combined with light massage were once prescribed in ancient Greece for patients who were in pain and also for the mentally disturbed:

> To soothe the nervous, the bed was hung as a cradle and rocked . . . sweet essences were rubbed on the patient's face or his feet, his head was stroked or he was scratched gently on the temple and around the ears. Music and gentle rocking both had a high place for nervous and irritable cases. (Nutting and Dock, 1907)

The close one-to-one relationship of carer and patient in these therapies often facilitates opportunities to learn of fears and hopes which otherwise would not be verbally expressed by the patient: apart from physical relief emotional needs can also be met.

THE KING'S TOUCH

A curious practice known as 'Touching for the King's Evil'

129

is commonly thought to have originated with Edward the Confessor (1066). The 'King's Evil' was a name given to 'scrofula', which apparently was a type of bovine tuberculosis, and which is still fairly common today in some parts of Europe. The kings of England and France were reputed to be invested with a royal touch. By stroking the afflicted area, they were able to heal the glandular disease. Malcolm, in Shakespeare's *Macbeth*, reflects on the healing properties of Edward's touch:

> Tis called the evil:
> A most miraculous work in this good king,
> Which often since my here – remain in England
> I have seen him do, how he solicits heaven
> Himself best knows; but strangely-visited people,
> All swollen and ulcerous, pitiful to the eye,
> The mere despair of surgery he cures,
> Hanging a golden stamp about their necks,
> Put on with holy prayers, and 'tis spoken,
> To the succeeding royalty he leaves
> The healing benediction.

(IV.III)

There is also attestation to 'Touching for the King's Evil' performed by Henry II, and an official ceremony was introduced by Henry VII in which the King laid his hands upon the sore of the sick person, who knelt before him while the chaplain recited the Gospel according to St Mark (16:18): '*Super aegros manus imponunt, et bene habebunt*' ('They shall lay hands on the sick and they shall recover'). Services for 'Touching' were used by Mary Tudor and her father, Henry VIII, Elizabeth I, and during the reigns of James I and Charles I. Gusmer (1974) records an entry in the diary of John Evelyn (d.1706) describing the enormous popularity of the 'Touching' in the reign of Charles II. It reads: 'Six or seven were crushed to death by pressing at the chirurgeon's door for tickets.' The service used by Charles II was reprinted in the 1662 edition of *The Book of Common Prayer* and positioned between the Commination and the Psalms. There is no evidence that the ceremony of touching was used during the reigns of William and Mary. Macaulay (1855), in his *History of England*, recalls that 'William had too much sense to be duped and too much honesty to bear a part in what he knew to be an imposture.' Writing in 1535 Servetus observes that 'The King [Francis I of France] himself by his touch cures those suffering from struma or scrofula', but concludes, 'I myself have seen the King touch many attacked by this ailment but I have never seen any cured.'

Not all the reactions were so unfavourable however. William Clowes (1602), a famous surgeon of his day, professed firm belief in the healing power of The King's Touch in his publication entitled, 'A right fruitefull and profitable treatise for the artificial cure of the malady called in Latin, *struma*, and in English, The Evill, cured by kinges and queenes of England'. Thomas Fuller, who as a youth had been present in Salisbury Cathedral and had witnessed the touch of James I, also professes unwavering faith: 'If any doubt of the truth thereof, they may be remitted to their own eyes for further confirmation.' He then asks: 'Shall we be so narrow-hearted as not to conceive it possible that Christian men, the noblest of corporeal creatures, kings, the most eminent of all Christian men, kings of Britain, the first-fruits of all Christian kings; should not receive the peculiar privilege and sanative power, whereof daily instances are presented unto us.'

The practice was renewed for the last time in England under Queen Anne (1702–1714). The healings were performed mostly in London (by Charles II at the Banqueting Hall, Whitehall), but the ceremony was possible wherever the Court might be. Easter, Whitsuntide and Michaelmas were the usual seasons, and the hot weather was avoided! Each applicant had to bring a certificate from the clergyman of his parish, and signatures of the churchwardens also were required by a proclamation issued in 1683. Sufferers were occasionally sent from various parts of the country at the partial cost of their parishes. For example, in 1682 the Corporation of Preston paid 10s for a bricklayer's son to go to London 'in order to the procuring of His Majesty's Touch'.

Some authentic healings undoubtedly took place, the majority probably due to 'suggestion'. Scrofula is not readily cured, but there can be temporary remissions. Those who were not healed were said to lack faith or told that the diagnosis was initially an incorrect one. The change of air involved in a journey to the Royal Court, religious solemnity, the expectant attention, even the belief in the touch-piece as an amulet, would all tend to help the natural curative process. 'While the practice did show some measure of concern for sick people in their infirmities,' concludes Gusmer, 'to say that the "Touching for the King's Evil" was a direct forerunner of the current healing ministry would be a gratuitous assumption.'

A GIFT OF HEALING

The laying on of hands to help or heal has been very much a part of all history. There are some persons who seem to be endowed with a 'gift' of healing who by the laying on of their hands are able to bring healing to certain sick and troubled people. It appears to be a 'power' inherent in certain people which emanates from them with beneficial effects upon the lives of others. It may be present without conscious desire or realization of need of it, and is quite often exercised apart from any profession of the Christian faith. While the power of suggestion may play a part in such cures, it does not wholly explain them. There appears to be no satisfactory rationale of this gift of healing through the laying on of hands (which should be distinguished from the gift possessed by the Apostles and Saints of the Christian Church). It may possibly be seen as the action of radiations, vibrations or of 'odic force'. In some instances it helps to mobilize the *medicatrix naturae vitae*, which is the body's natural recuperative powers. Many 'cures' claimed by healers are of self-limiting conditions which have a large psychosomatic element in their aetiology, and validation of the healing in these instances presents a problem. One of the disturbing factors is that certain 'healers' are apt to make exaggerated and unsubstantiated claims of 'miraculous cures'.

There is a body of belief within Spiritualism that the spirits of departed persons (usually 'spirit doctors') are able to transmit a wide range of healing through the laying on of hands. The 'healer' is seen as a 'medium' of healing, which is conveyed through the influence of disembodied spirits, many of whom were well-known physicians of their time (e.g. Lister and Pasteur).

Healers have differing viewpoints as to the nature and

source of the interplay of energy and healing between 'healer' and patient. There have been various experiments carried out to promote, if possible, clear scientific evidence of the reality of a gift of healing by means of the laying on of hands, for such healing energy is not detectable by any conventional measuring instruments. One of the earliest examples of such research was carried out in the early and mid sixties. Bernard Grad (1961, 1964), a Canadian biochemist, with the cooperation of a renowned healer, Oskar Estebany, conducted double-blind studies on mice and barley-seeds. Three hundred mice with back wounds were randomly assigned to one experimental or one of two control groups. The researchers report that 'mice were selected because their small size enabled us to meet the demands of present-day biomedical and statistical techniques to utilize sufficiently large numbers of animals and yet not exceed the modest space and funds available for their housing and feeding.' The experimental group was treated by a 'healer'. A hundred mice in a metal holder were touched by the healer's hands for fifteen minutes, morning and evening, five times a week. The second group of one hundred was treated by medical students who claimed no paranormal healing abilities; the other group received no treatment at all. It was later found that the 'healer' accelerated significantly the rate of wound healing in the mice in the first group, as compared with those in the control groups. Evidence was also obtained that body heat could not be invoked as the cause of the accelerated healing.

Subsequent studies involved tests on the effects of the laying on of hands on the growth of barley seeds, which were soaked in a saline solution to simulate a 'sick' condition. As with the experiments on mice, so, too, the seedlings were divided into groups. The first control group was watered by tap water, the second by water from flasks held by disinterested persons, and the third (experimental group) was watered by flasks held by Estebany. This latter group of seeds sprouted more quickly, grew taller and had more chlorophyll than the seeds in the control groups!

In the late sixties another biochemist and enzymologist, Sr M. Justa Smith, carried out further research on the laying on of hands. Her basic assumption was 'that if an energy change occurs during healing, from whatever means, the change should be apparent at the enzymatic level, for it is the enzymes that are crucial to the basal metabolism of the body' (Kreiger, 1975). Her conclusions were that the healer's ability does not affect all enzymes the same way – in fact, some are not affected at all. However, within the context of what enzymes do in the human body, the substantive effects all seem to contribute to improving or maintaining health (Smith, 1972). Research has also been carried out by means of Kirlian photography which is reputed to capture the 'halo' of energy around living matter (Krippner and Rubin, 1973).

A recent Dutch study undertaken by Beutler (1988) on paranormal healing and hypertension observed whether paranormal healing by laying on of hands might reduce blood pressure in essential hypertension, and whether such an effect might be due to a paranormal, psychological or placebo factor. Patients (120 participants) were randomized to three treatment groups: paranormal healing by laying on of hands, paranormal healing at a distance, and no paranormal healing. It was concluded that paranormal healing is safe in complementary medicine but there is little evidence of the effect of a paranormal factor. The fall in blood pressure in all three groups was probably caused by the psychosocial approach or was a placebo effect of the trial itself.

THERAPEUTIC TOUCH

Influenced by the studies of Grad (1961, 1964) and Smith (1972) Kreiger began research on touch in human beings relating to 'fields' and 'energy flow' in and around a patient's body. Her technique known as 'therapeutic touch' has received growing attention and use (Kreiger 1972, 1974, 1975). It has been termed the 'imprimatur of nursing' by Kreiger who defines the procedure thus:

> The therapeutic use of hands . . . appears to be a universal human act; however, it is an act that we have all but forgotten in this scientific age in our adulation of things mechanical, synthetic and, frequently, anti-human. Therapeutic touch has recaptured this simple but elegant mode of healing and mated it with the rigour and power of modern science. . . .

134

The act consists of the simple placing of the hands for about 10–15 minutes on, or close to, the body of an ill person, by someone who intends to help or to heal that person. It is 'a method of healing derived from, but not the same as, the laying on of hands.' It is not associated with any specific religious belief and is not carried out within a religious context. Kreiger turned to concepts of Eastern philosophy for a conceptual rationale, and viewed human health as an expression of an essential energy system called *prana* (which in English might be translated as 'vitality'). Eastern literature states that the healthy person has a superabundance of *prana* and that those who are sick have a deficit. An interchange of vitality is reputed to occur when a healthy person purposefully touches an ill person with a strong intent to help or to heal. Therapeutic touch was introduced by Kreiger as a response to the increase of technology in today's modern health care system. 'I know that when I lay my hands on or near an ill person,' states Kreiger, 'he has a subjective sense of heat in the area that is ill or diseased, a sense of relaxation and wellbeing . . . it can also be stated that faith on the part of the subject does not make a significant difference in the healing effect.'

The act of therapeutic touch consists of various stages: centring, assessment, and energy transfer. In the initial phase the carer tries to develop a sense of deep internal stillness or meditative state, along with an intent to heal. In the second stage the carer or healer moves his or her hands several inches above the patient's body. As these hand movements continue the healer becomes aware of sensations such as heat, cold, tingling and pressure. These sensations are then interpreted as revealing the condition of the patient. Diagnosis is formulated over these areas of the body which seem to need energy. It is then held that energy is transmitted through the healer's hands into the body of the patient.

Therapeutic touch is seen as a holistic nursing intervention. Its usefulness appears to have been applicable in instances of acute and chronic pain (Witt, 1984: Keller, 1986): in reducing anxiety in post-myocardial patients (Heldt, 1981): during labour and delivery (Kreiger, 1983), and in the reduction of stress in premature babies (Fedoruk, 1980).

There appears to be no proof of the efficacy of therapeutic

touch yet elaborate theories have been developed of how it works. Boguslawski (1979) and Kreiger (1979) advocate that therapeutic touch is a communication or transfer of energy from the healer to the patient. Theoretical concepts such as *prana*, 'life energy' and 'energy field' are employed in current literature on therapeutic touch but no adequate definitions of these concepts are provided.

The appropriateness of therapeutic touch as a nursing intervention has been questioned (Walike, 1975: Levine, 1979: Curtin, 1980) and research investigating its effects has been criticized (Gottfried, 1984: Smith, 1984: Clark, 1984). Although interest in the procedure has grown in the USA and it is now being taught in 50 universities, there is still relatively little controlled research on therapeutic touch and none is at present taking place in the United Kingdom (it is however in use in the Bristol Cancer Help Centre). One study undertaken by Kreiger (1976) claimed an increase in hemoglobin levels during the immediate post-operative period. As the study involved only a small number of patients without a control group, the findings have been subject to question (Clark and Clark, 1984). Another study conducted by Heidt (1981) compared the effect on anxiety-reduction of therapeutic touch, casual touch and simple conversation. There was found to be a significant reduction with therapeutic touch in both pre- and post-treatment anxiety. Here again it is impossible to determine whether the reported reduction in anxiety was due to an hypothesized transfer of energy or to a placebo effect. The current research base supporting continued nursing practice of therapeutic touch is, at best, weak, conclude Clark and Clark (1984). It appears to need far more effective and stringent research, for at present there is no sufficient evidence either for or against the view that therapeutic touch has therapeutic effects beyond those of a placebo. It is thought that some aspects of therapeutic touch energy-interaction are highly developed forms of love, empathy and caring.

THE CHURCH'S MINISTRY OF HEALING

The Church's ministry of healing is entirely independent of and distinct from any natural, psychic or paranormal abilities.

The laying on of hands is seen as a sacramental act, a blessing conveying peace and confidence to a sick person, and is by no means an isolated act of one who claims to be a healer with a special 'gift'. Rather is it the 'applying' of a community's love and sympathy. Much of its efficacy is derived from the worshipping community itself. 'When the minister lays his hand upon the head of a sick person, it is as if the hands of all the congregation are with his hands, focussing their love and prayer for the one in need. It is a corporate act of the Church as the Christ-indwelt community' (Wilson, 1966). As an act of the Church the laying on of hands, well authenticated by both Scripture and tradition, has been used to convey power and authority. The most frequent means of healing used by Christ himself were speaking words and touching the sick person with his hand. Sometimes the two were combined, but on occasions they were used separately. In the later history of the Church 'touch' became known as a 'laying on of hands'.

In the Old Testament the laying on of hands is associated with:

1. *Commissioning*. It is used by Moses in his commissioning of Joshua (Num. 27:18, 23), 'And the Lord said unto Moses, "Take thee Joshua, the son of Nun, a man in whom is the spirit, and lay thine hand upon him. . . ." and he laid his hands upon him, and he gave him a charge. . .' (cf. Deut. 34:9).

2. An act of *Blessing and Healing*. Jacob blesses his grand-children by laying hands upon them (Gen. 48:14). Elisha places his hands upon a sick child to heal him (2 Kings 4:34), 'And he went up, and lay upon the child, and he put his mouth upon his mouth, and his eyes upon his eyes, and his hands upon his hands: and he stretched himself upon the child; and the flesh of the child waxed warm.' Elijah stretched himself three times upon the widow's dead son (1 Kings 17:21).

3. An act of *Dedication*. The people of Israel lay hands on the Levites in order that they may be dedicated (Num. 8:10), 'And the children of Israel shall put their hands upon the Levites. . . .'

4. An act of *Sacrifice*. The imposition of hands is used for

137

the sins being put upon the scapegoat on the Day of Atonement (Lev. 16:21), 'And Aaron shall lay both his hands upon the head of the live goat, and confess over him all the iniquities of the children of Israel . . . putting them upon the head of the goat. . . .' Hands are also lent on an animal to be sacrificed (Exod. 29:10,15,19; 2 Chron. 29:33; Lev. 1:4, 4:15).

5. An act of *Punishment of Blasphemy*. The witnesses lay their hand on the offender and say to the people, 'whosoever curseth his God shall bear his sin.' Headley (1988) notes that 'there is the sense of putting back onto the accused any taint of associated guilt before the execution.'

Touch in the New Testament has a deeper significance. There is *blessing* (Matt. 19:13; Lk. 24:50–51; Acts 1:8–9), *healing* (Mk. 5:23; 7:32; 16:18; Acts 9:12), *baptizing* (Mk 10:16; Acts 8:17–19) and *commissioning* (Acts 6:6; 13:3). The majority of the New Testament references to touch or the laying on of hands, unlike those found in the Old Testament, come in the context of *healing*. The laying on of hands formed an essential element of the healing ministry of Jesus as well as that of the Apostolic Church. The following outline lists the works of healing recorded in the Gospels in which touch is used:

HEALING	METHOD	MATT.	MARK	LUKE
1 Peter's wife's mother	Touch, word: prayer of friends	8:14	1:30	4:38
2 Multitudes	Touch, word: faith of friends	8:16	1:32	4:40
3 A leper	Word, touch: leper's faith and Christ's compassion	8:2	1:40	5:12
4 Jairus' daughter	Word, touch: faith of father	9:18	5:22	8:41
5 Woman with issue of blood	Touching his garment in faith	9:20	5:25	8:43
6 A few sick folk	Touch (hindered by unbelief)	13:58	6:5	

138

HEALING	METHOD	MATT.	MARK	LUKE
7 Multitudes	Touch of his garments, friends' faith	14:34	6:55	
8 Deaf and dumb man	Word, touch: friends' prayer			7:32
10 Blind Bartimaeus	Word, touch, compassion, faith	20:30	10:46	18:35
11 Two blind men	Word, touch: men's faith	9:27		
12 Woman bound by Satan	Word, touch			13:10
13 Man with dropsy	Touch			14:1
14 Malchus' ear	Touch			22:49

It is interesting to note that Jesus never touched persons who appeared to be demon-possessed (Mk. 5:1–20; Matt. 8:28–34; Lk. 4:33–37; Matt. 9:32–33).

The Greek verb used of Jesus 'touching' or 'being touched' implies a touch which tends to hold and even sometimes to cling. We may assume therefore that Jesus literally held the leper and was not quick to withdraw contact from him (Matt. 8:3; Mk. 1:41; Lk. 5:12). It is likely too that he gripped the hand of Peter's wife's mother (Matt. 8:15). A different verb is used to signify 'handling' or 'feeling', as in searching for something, when Jesus invited the Eleven to 'handle' him after his resurrection (Lk. 24:39).

In the Acts of the Apostles there are six instances of touch being used, two involving the laying on of hands (9:17–19, Ananias lays hands on Saul in his blindness; 28:7–10, the father of Publius is healed of his fever by Paul). The remaining instances are not specifically laying on of hands for healing, but rather initiation and the giving of the Spirit (e.g. 8:17, Peter and John at Samaria), commissioning (13:3, Barnabas and Saul) and ordination (6:6, seven deacons, c.f. 1 Tim. 4:14; 5:22). After Pentecost the laying on of hands especially denoted the conferral of the power and authority of the episcopacy which Christ had given to the Apostles.

In the Apostolic age the ministry of healing was not meant

to terminate with the resurrection and ascension of our Lord. The laying on of hands for purposes of healing has always been continued in the Christian Church. The nineteen works of healing recorded in the Acts of the Apostles illustrate how 'many signs and wonders were wrought by the hands of the Apostles', as a consequence of fulfilling the injunction of our Lord to heal in his name. In the Apostolic age the power to heal was a gift of the Spirit (1 Cor. 12:9): it was one among other gifts (v.11): it was not given to all (v.30): it was one of the greater gifts, and as such was to be sought for (v.3): its chief object was the common good (v.7), and the royal road to its attainment was love (v.31).

The laying on of hands has always been closely interwoven with the history of holy unction. Indeed unction was frequently referred to as *impositio manum* in the mediaeval offices of Milan, and probably also by St Ambrose (*De Poenitentia* 1.8), St Augustine (*Vita* 27) and St Athanasius (*Epistola Cyclica*). It also became a necessary part of Christian Initiation, but being connected with anointing its place tended to be taken by the latter in some Churches.

The laying on of hands is also used in benedictions (in individual benedictions the gesture is that of hands placed on the head (Gen. 48:13,14; Matt. 19:13): in more general benedictions it is that of the raised and open hand or hands, as if to project the blessing forward upon the persons or objects to be blessed), in visitation of the sick, absolution and, in earlier times, and in the Eastern Church still as well as in some Western Churches, at the unction in holy Baptism. At the consecration of bishops, bishops alone may lay on their hands; at the ordination of priests, the bishop lays on his hands together with the other priests present. Hands are laid on in order to transmit strengthening, healing and consecrating power from Christ to his Church.

In the 'Alternative Services: Ministry to the Sick, authorized pursuant to Canon B2 of the Canons of the Church of England', an explanation of the laying on of hands is given as follows:

Our Lord Jesus Christ went about preaching the gospel and healing. He commanded his disciples to lay hands on the sick that they might be healed. Following his example,

and in obedience to his command, we shall lay hands on
N, praying that the Lord will grant healing and peace
according to his loving and gracious will.

At the actual laying on of hands the following or other suitable
words are used:

In the name of our Lord Jesus Christ who laid his hands
on the sick that they might be healed, *I* lay *my* hands upon
you, *N*. May Almighty God, Father, Son and Holy Spirit,
make you whole in body, mind and spirit, give you light
and peace, and keep you in life eternal. Amen.

In sickness physical touch can be seen as an antidote to fear
and anxiety, freeing and mobilizing the body's natural healing
and calming the troubled mind and spirit. The laying on of
hands is no magical gesture. It is a sacramental act of much
spiritual significance. It is to be used in full co-operation with
both doctor and nurse for each is concerned with the patient
as a person, and for the wholeness of his being. In an age of
high and sophisticated technology the gentle human touch of
the hands of the doctor, the nurse, the priest, the carer, the
helper or the friend is needed as perhaps never before.

Touch is essentially the sign and sense of love *par excellence*,
and in order to find the profound meaning of touch we must
see it from the point of view of love. When an outward and
human touch becomes transformed by an inward and divine
love, it is then, and then only, that we are able to bring solace
to the sad, strength to the weak and healing to the sick.

Beutler, J. J., et al.	'Paranormal healing and hypertension', *Brit. Med. J.*, 296 (1988), pp. 1491–1494.
Boguslawski, M.	'Therapeutic touch: a facilitator of pain relief', *TCN/Pain Management* (1980), pp. 27–37.
	'The use of therapeutic touch in nursing', *J. Cont. Educ. Nurs.*, 10:4 (1979), pp. 9–15.
Clark, P. E., and Clark, M. J.	'Therapeutic touch: is there a scientific basis for practice?' *Nursing Research*, 33:1 (1984), pp. 37–41.

Curtin, L. — 'Nurse quackery', *Supervisor Nurse*, 12 (1980), p. 9.

Evelyn, J. — *The Diary*, ed. W. Bray, (Vol. 1). Everyman's Library 1936, p. 343.

Fedoruk, R. B. — 'Transfer of the relaxation response: therapeutic touch as a method for reduction of stress in premature neonates' (Unpublished Doctoral Dissertation). University of Maryland 1980.

Fuller, T. — In *Church History*, ed. J. S. Brewer. Oxford 1845, pp. 387–390.

Gottfried, A., and Reite, M. — 'Discussion, pediatric round table 10: touch', in *The Many Facets of Touch*, eds C. C. Brown and N. J. Skillman. Johnson & Johnson 1984, pp. 149–172.

Grad, B. — 'A telekinetic effect on plant growth. Part 2. Experiments involving treatment of saline in stoppered bottles', *Int. J. Parapsychol.*, 6 (1964), pp. 473–498.
'Some biological effects of the "Laying on of Hands": a review of experiments with animals and plants', *J. Amer. Soc. for Psychical Research*, 59 (1964), p. 95.

Grad, B., et al. — 'The influence of an unorthodox method of treatment on wound healing in mice', *Int. J. Parapsychol.*, 3 (1961), pp. 5–24.

Gusmer, C. W. — *The Ministry of Healing in the Church of England: An Ecumenical-Liturgical Study*, The Alcuin Club. Mayhew-McCrimmon, Great Wakering 1974, pp. 86–90.

Headley, C. — *The Laying on of Hands in the Parish Healing Ministry* (Grove Worship Series, No. 104). Grove Books Ltd 1988.

Heidt, P. — 'Effect of therapeutic touch on anxiety level of hospitalized patients', *Nursing Research*, 30 (1981), pp. 32–37.

Keller, E., and Bzdek, V. M. — 'Effects of therapeutic touch on tension headache pain', *Nursing Research*, 35:2 (1986), pp. 101–106.

Kreiger, D. — 'Therapeutic touch: the imprimatur of nursing', *Amer. J. Nurs.*, 75 (1975), pp. 784–787.

'The response of in-vivo hemoglobin to an active healing therapy by direct laying on of hands', *Hum. Dimensions*, 1 (1972), pp. 12–15.

'The relationship of touch, with intent to help or to heal, to subjects' in-vivo hemoglobin values: a study in personalized interaction', Paper presented at the American Nurses' Association Ninth Nursing Research Conference, held at San Antonio, Texas, 21–23 March 1973.

'Healing by the laying-on of hands as a facilitator of bioenergetic change: the response of in-vivo human hemoglobin', *Psychoenergetic Systems*, 1 (1976), pp. 121–129.

'Kreiger presents childbirth study at therapeutic touch research day', *Co-operative Connection Newsletter of the Nurse Healers, Professional Associates, Inc.*, 4:2 (1983), pp. 1–2.

Krippner, S., and Rubin, D., (eds)   *Galaxies of Life*. Gordon and Breach, New York 1973.

Levine, M. E.   Corres. *American Journal of Nursing*, 79:8 (1979), pp. 1379–1381.

Nouwen, H.   Personal communication (1988).

Nutting, A., and Dock, L. L.   *A History of Nursing*. G. P. Putnam & Sons, Knickerbocker Press, New York 1907, p. 81.

Servetos, M.   Observations added to his 1535 Ed. of Ptolemy's Geography. Trs. C. D. O'Malley, in Michael Servetus I.

Smith, J.   'A critical appraisal of therapeutic touch', in *The Many Facets of Touch*, eds. C. C. Brown and N. J. Skillman. Johnson & Johnson 1984, pp. 156–162.

Smith, Sister M.   'Paranormal effects on enzyme activity', *Hum. Dimensions*, 1 (1972), pp. 15–19.

Walike, B. C., et al.   Corres. *American Journal of Nursing*, 75:8 (1975), pp. 1278–9.

Wilson, M.   *The Church is Healing*. SCM Press, London 1966.

Witt, J. R.   'Relieving chronic pain', *Nurse Practitioner*, 9:1 (1984), pp. 36–38.

Epilogue

In the room at l'Arche where portions of this book were written hangs an icon: a reproduction of the famous Byzantine icon of the Vladimir Mother of God, belonging to the late eleventh or the early twelfth century. The original was brought to Kiev from Constantinople and is now in the Tretiakov Gallery.

The icon is venerated as the greatest holy treasure of the Russian nation. The distinctive feature of the Vladimir icon of the Mother of God is the posture of herself and the Holy Child, whom she holds in her right arm, bending her head towards him. With her left hand she either touches the Child's shoulders or holds him to her breast, prayerfully extending her hand to him and at the same time directing the spectator's attention to him. The hands of Mary form the centre-piece of the whole icon.

Mother and Child sum up for us the mystery of the Incarnation, of the Word made flesh. It is St John who speaks to us of the Incarnation: 'The Word was made flesh, and dwelt among us, (and we beheld his glory, the glory as of the only begotten of the Father,) full of grace and truth' (1:14). God sent us his Son not principally in order to give us his Word; rather the great mystery of Christianity is the relationship between the Word and *the body*. Throughout the vision of Jesus the body takes on a most important role: 'Destroy this temple, and in three days I will raise it up. Then said the Jews, Forty and six years was this temple in building, and wilt thou rear it up in three days? But he spake of the temple

144

of his body' (John 2:19–21). The body of Christ is the place in which resides the divinity: the body of Christ is the place where God dwells.

God sent his Son in order that we may touch God and that God may touch us. In all the miracles of Christ we see the link between touch and the Word. He touches the eyes of the blind man, and he touches the leper, and says that they are clean. It is touch and the Word: the body and the Word – the realization of a new form of touch. When we touch people, particularly those who are sick or handicapped, we want that touch to be a touch that is life-giving: a touch that gives security and peace. When we are consciously touching people or holding people in order to give them security, in order that they might discover that they are loved, that touch, as the Word, can become – and does become – an instrument of grace.

The message of the Vladimir icon reveals to us a profound truth – that we may touch God and God may touch us. God himself always touches us but what is extraordinary is that we can touch God: we ourselves may have the possibility of coming very close to God. It is this that makes touch of all gifts the most precious.

Index of Proper Names

Abram, H. S. 46
Amacher, N. 54
Anderson, D. 35
Anisfield, E. 33
Aquilera, D. 97
Ardrey, R. 42
Argyle, M. 18, 36
Aristotle ix
Ashton, J. x
Ashworth, P. 54, 74, 83

Bacorn, C. N. 91, 93
Balint, M. 35
Ballard, K. 76
Barker, R. K. 76
Barnard, K. E. 71
Barnett, K. 4, 44, 51, 53, 76, 100, 110
Beard, F. W. 72
Beese, J. xi
Benfield, D. G. 67
Benoliel, J. Q. 78
Bertodano, T. de xii
Bettman, O. L. 60
Beutler, J. J. 134
Birdwhistell, R. L. 10
Blackburn, S. N. 71
Boguslawski, M. 136
Boon, S. 75
Bowlby, J. 31, 41, 66, 76
Breu, D. 83
Breuer, J. 89
Brodsky, A. 93
Bronowski, J. 55

Brown, R. 18
Bruhn, J. G. 56
Buber, M. 3
Burnside, I. M. 47, 109–10
Burton, A. 9, 26, 78, 98
Burton, R. 63
Byass, R. 122
Bzdek, V. M. 135

Caplan, G. 63
Carlson, D. 77
Cashar, L. 92
Cassidy, S. 116
Celsus 79
Charles-Edwards, A. 54
Chatterton, P. 122
Clark, M. J. 136
Clark, P. E. 136
Clynes, M. 14
Cohen, J. 90
Cope, G. 112
Corless, I. x
Critchley, M. 6, 10
Curson, M. 57
Curtin, L. 136

Darwin, C. 15
Davis, F. 111
de Augustinis, J. 98
de Meyer, J. 76
de Wever, M. K. 110
Dickson, D. 10
Dixon, B. K. 91
Dixon, D. N. 93

Dock, L. L. 129
Dominian, J. 40–1
Dominica, F. xi
Doyle, D. xi, 58, 120
Dracup, K. 83
Drayton, M. xi
Duff, R. S. 41
Duhamel, T. R. 69
Durr, C. A. 48, 51
Dye, A. 92

Ekman, P. 111
Elonen, A. S. 7
Engel, G. L. 28
English, S. 10
Erikson, E. H. 33, 35
Evans, D. 100
Evelyn, J. 130

Farrah, S. J. 13, 48–9, 98
Fedoruk, R. B. 135
Feifel, H. 114
Fernsler, J. 76
Field, T. M. 69
Fisher, J. D. 4, 13, 18, 52
Fleck, S. 42
Forer, B. R. 92
Frank, L. K. 6, 24, 27
Freud, A. 33
Freud, S. 9, 89, 123
Frieson, W. 111
Fromm-Reichmann, F. 94
Fuller, T. 131

Gantt, W. H. 80
Garrity, T. F. 74
Gibbon, B. 83
Gillie, O. 68
Gilman, A. 18
Goffman, E. 18, 42
Goodyear, R. K. 91
Goodykoontz, L. 44
Gottfried, A. W. 69, 136
Grad, B. 133–4
Grant, G. P. 86

Greenberg, B. M. 109
Greenwald, H. 36
Gries, M. L. 76
Gusmer, C. W. 132

Hackett, T. P. 113
Hall, E. T. 11, 15, 44
Hampe, S. O. 83
Hargie, O. 10
Harlow, H. F. 30
Headley, C. 138
Heidt, P. 136
Heller, L. G. 26, 78, 98
Henderson, V. 75
Henley, N. M. 18, 44
Henley, W. E. 98
Heylings, P. N. K. 8, 57
Heyter, J. 43
Hill, S. 72–3
Hinton, J. xi
Hippocrates 129
Hoffman, A. 100
Hollingshead, A. B. 41
Holbert, D. 52
Hollinger, L. M. 110
Holroyd, J. 93
Hooker, D. 24
Hopkins, J. xi
Howe, R. 59
Hull, R. x
Hurtt, B. L. 113
Huss, A. J. 14, 46, 78

Johnson, B. S. 10, 45, 47, 97
Jones, E. 90, 92
Jourard, S. M. 5–9, 35, 50, 91, 95, 111

Kaplan, D. M. 64
Keane, V. R. 24
Kees, W. 5
Keller, E. 135
Keller, H. 19
Kennell, J. H. 25–6, 33–4, 36, 66, 72

Klaus, M. H. x, 25–6, 29, 33–4,
   36, 66, 72
Klein, M. 11
Klein, R. F. 74
Knable, J. 76
Kravitz, H. 23
Kreiger, D. 134–6
Krippner, S. 134
Kubler-Ross, E. xi, 116

Laing, R. D. 9
Lamb, C. 43
Langland, R. M. 47
Laycock, T. 56
Lazarus, R. S. 77
Leboyer, F. 32
Lesser, M. S. 24
Levine, M. E. 136
Levine, S. 16
Lewis, C. S. 124
Lewis, M. 8
Lichter, I. xi, 117–18, 121–2
Liley, A. W. 23
Lindemann, E. 63, 123
Lipper, E. 33
Lowen, A. 99
Lucente, F. E. 42
Lugton, J. x
Lust, B. 84
Lynch, J. J. 78, 80

Macdonald, J. 70
Mackereth, P. A. 75
Marmer, J. 103
Marsh, B. T. 42
Mason, E. 64
May, R. 41
Mayerson, E. W. 73
Mayne, M. 40, 57
Mazis, G. A. 12
McClelland, W. J. 16
McCorkie, R. 47, 75
Mead, M. 46
Menninger, K. 90
Mercer, L. S. 48, 97

Meredith, S. 48
Miles, M. S. 70
Minckley, B. 43
Mintz, L. E. 9, 90, 92, 103
Montagu, A. 5–6, 16, 24, 27–9,
   33, 99, 108
Morgan, C. xi
Morris, D. 11–12, 16, 56
Morse, J. M. 78
Moss, A. A. 53

Neisser, U. ix
Newton, J. E. D. 80
Norberg, A. 100
Nouwen, H. x, 59, 102
Nutting, A. 129

Older, J. 55, 59, 89, 93, 103,
   116
Osler, W. 43

Panicucci, C. L. 47
Parkes, C. M. xi, 114, 123, 125
Patterson, M. 13
Pattinson, J. E. 91
Penny, K. S. 24
Philip, A. E. 77
Pluckham, M. L. 7
Pollack, C. B. 96
Powell, L. F. 71
Prugh, D. 68

Rapoport, L. 63
Redfern, S. 75
Reichsman, F. 28
Revesz, G. 19
Robertiello, R. 92, 99
Rogers, C. 104
Rosen, J. 16
Rosenblatt, P. C. 125
Rubin, D. 134
Rubin, S. E. 8, 32–5
Ruesch, J. 5

Sapir, E. 3

Sartre J.-P. 3
Saunders, C. 10
Schilder, P. 33
Schmahl, J. A. 77
Seaman, L. 127
Sechehaye, M. 99
Servetos, M. 143
Sims, S. 122
Sleath, K. 67
Smith, J. 133–4
Smith, M. Sr. 134
Spiegel, R. 107
Spitz, R. 28
Steele, B. 96
Stockwell, S. R. 92
Stubblefield, H. W. 101
Suiter, R. L. 91

Tatebaum, J. 124
Taylor, A. xii
Taylor, J. 112
Tobiason, S. J. B. 108
Tolstoy, L. 119, 123
Twycross, R. xi

Vanier, J. x, 101–2
Vanier, T. x, 102
Velde, S. Van de 78

Walike, B. C. 136
Walker, D. N. 44
Watson, W. H. 46, 53
Watson, S. 70
Weininger, O. 16
Weisman, A. D. 113
Weiss, S. J. 13, 78
Westman, J. C. 53
Whitby, C. 71
Whitcher, S. J. 52
Whitelaw, A. 67
Wilkes, E. xi
Wilson, J. M. 94–6
Wilson, M. 137
Winnicott, D. W. 29, 31, 33
Witt, J. R. 135
Wolberg, L. 90, 92

Young, M. G. 8, 42

General Index

abandonment 99–100, 123–5
absolution 140
abstinence 90
acceptance 58–9, 91, 100,
    102–4, 109–11, 115–18
act, sacramental 137, 141
administrators 41
adolescence 12, 14, 17, 36, 44
adults 12, 16
affection 7, 10
aged 51, 54, 98, 108–11
amniotic fluid 24
anaesthesia 43–4
analysts 90–7
anger 12, 41, 67, 79, 90, 94, 97,
    102, 115
anxiety 12, 25, 40–3, 45, 48, 63,
    67, 74, 80, 93–4, 99, 101,
    113, 117, 136, 141
arrhythmia, cardiac 80
assessment 44, 84, 122, 135
attachment 23, 31, 34–6, 124–5

baby 23–35
baby, premature xi, 64–73, 135
baptisms 37
beauticians 18, 122
bedside manner, 55, 78
benediction 56–7, 98, 118
bereavement 59, 108, 121–6
birth 23–7, 32–5
blasphemy 138
bleeps 73
blessing 56–7, 98, 118

blind 18–19
body contact 4, 7, 9, 11, 31, 56
    guide 11
    image 25, 33, 95, 115, 122
    language 10, 99, 117
bonding 11, 23, 27, 31, 33, 66,
    68
bradycardia 77–8
braille 18–19
brain-damage 100, 109
breast 25, 66, 68, 70
breast feeding 26–7, 69

caesarean section 25
cancer 115, 122
care, pastoral 57–9, 112–16,
    119–21
carers, professional, x, 40–2,
    44–5, 47–9, 73–6, 78,
    112–13, 115, 117–22
caress 7, 17, 24–7, 31–2
castes 7
cats 8, 15
chaplains, hospital 44, 57–9,
    119
chemotherapy 116
child-abuse 36, 96–7
child, battered 36
childhood 23, 29–37
children 4, 8, 11–12, 28, 35, 37,
    43, 53, 84, 99
client 91–7, 103
closeness 12, 17–18, 36, 97–8,
    109

cognition 29
comfort 30, 41, 44, 49–50, 120–2
communication 3–4, 9, 11–13, 23, 27, 42, 45, 47, 74, 83, 99–100, 116–19
  non-verbal 4, 9–11, 31, 45, 47, 74, 76, 95, 99–100, 109, 114–18
  oral, 12, 27, 42, 49–50, 95, 124
commissioning 137
companionship 25, 46–9, 118–20
compassion 4, 46, 57, 84, 112
Compassionate Friends 123
contact, cutaneous 24–7, 31, 58–9, 65
  physical 11–19, 23–7, 32–7, 40, 42–4, 57–9, 64–6, 84, 89–91, 97–104
contractions 24–5
conversation, pastoral 59
counselling 5, 89–104
counsellor 89–97
countertransference 104
cot-sides 110
crisis 63, 76–84, 95
cuddle 28–30, 114, 124–5
culture 4, 6–7, 9–10, 27, 35

death 41, 71–3, 109, 123–6
dedication 137
dementia 100
demon-possession 139
denial 10, 27, 40, 103
dentists 18
dependency 44, 48, 52, 92, 102–3, 110, 124
depersonalization 9, 46, 109, 118, 122
depression 28, 40, 74, 92–3, 95, 115
deprivation 35–6, 64–5, 68–9, 77–9
detachment 99

development, human 31
disease 95–6, 108
disintegration 40, 47, 113
disorientation 13, 108
distancing 5, 11–12, 41, 58, 102, 114
doctors 17–18, 44, 59, 66, 71, 75, 77, 141
doctor-patient relationships 55–7, 115–16
dogs 8, 15, 80
dying 13, 71–3, 112–23

embrace 12, 37, 91, 103
embryo 24
empathy 4–5, 48–9, 53, 58, 77–9, 84, 104, 121, 136
energy flow 63, 133–5
  transfer 135–6
environment 32
enzymes 133–4
eye contact 17, 109, 116

family 6, 41–2, 83–4, 108–9, 118, 120, 125
fantasies 40–1, 67
fetus 23–4
friends 4, 42, 56
friendship 10, 59, 102
funeral director 126
funeral rites 125–6

geriatric chairs 110
gestation 24
gestures 3, 6, 10, 12, 16, 18, 44–5, 47, 54, 59, 92, 96, 99, 103, 110–11, 119, 140
girls 29, 36
graduations 37
grandchildren 108–9
grandparents 108
grief 13, 46, 59, 71–3, 83, 93, 121, 123–6
  anticipatory 36, 64, 83, 121
  work 124–5

groups, encounter 17–18
  sensitivity 17–18
guilt 44, 67, 83

hair-dressers 18, 109
handicapped, mental x, 1, 12,
    100, 102
  physical 1, 12, 28, 100, 102
hands 3, 7, 11–13, 16, 23, 32,
    35, 40, 46, 51, 63, 75, 92,
    124, 134, 144
  clasping 100, 123
  holding 1–2, 11, 13, 16, 40,
    47, 52, 54, 58–9, 76–7, 97,
    112, 116–17, 119, 121, 123
  laying on of 7, 46, 56–7, 114,
    137–41
handshake 4, 8, 11–12, 16, 37,
    55, 57, 93–4, 98, 101, 109,
    125
healer 55, 132–4
healing 4, 56, 95, 122–3, 129–41
  gift of 132–4
  ministry of 136–41
  paranormal 132–4
health 43, 53, 55, 73, 95, 102,
    116, 133–4
heart-beat 24–5
heart-rate 78–83
helplessness 41, 83, 109
hemoglobin 136
holding 30–1, 99
homeostasis 5, 32, 46
hospices xi, 48, 80, 114, 122,
    125
hospital 28, 40, 46, 53, 57, 110
  psychiatric 98
hospitalization 26, 29, 41, 46
hugs 16–17, 30, 53, 109, 114,
    121, 124
hypertension 134
hypnosis 9
hysteria 89

icon 144

identification 43, 58, 78, 95, 99,
    101, 112, 116
incubator 65–8, 70
infancy 23, 25–37
inferiority 45
insecurity 40, 113
intimacy 3, 8–9, 11, 35–6, 46,
    94, 99, 102, 114
isolation 116
isolette 64–5

King's Touch 129–32
  Evil 129
kissing 7, 11, 53, 103, 109, 115

labour 24–5, 32
laying on of hands 7, 46, 55, 57,
    78, 114, 137–41
leukemia 116
life-cycle 23–37
listening 10, 56, 115, 124
loneliness 13, 25, 36, 42, 45, 48,
    76, 109, 111, 124
love 10, 14, 25, 30, 32, 42, 95,
    101, 111, 119, 137, 145

magic 7–9
marasmus 27–8
marriage 37
massage 9, 17, 26, 29, 32, 34,
    66, 68, 102, 122, 129
masseurs 18
memories 9, 29, 94
microscope 56
midwife 32
ministers x, 57–9, 136–41
modalities 4, 10, 35, 96
monitors 73
monkeys 15, 29–30
mother-love 8, 12, 23–37, 65–73
mourning 123–6
movements, body 10–11
music 100, 102
myocardial infarction 77–80

neonate 25–7, 65–73
new-born 25–34
non-verbal 9–11, 46
nurses 24, 40, 44–51, 59, 68–84,
    97–8, 114–22, 141

odic force 132
oscillations 73–83

paediatrician 67
pain 13, 25, 47–8, 51, 58, 78,
    112, 135
parents 4, 7–8, 12, 36, 96–7
pastoral care 57–9
pastors 57–9, 136–41
patient 24, 41–58, 64–84,
    97–104, 134–6
    AIDS 54
    unconscious 13, 54
personnel, health 41, 53, 57
physician 32, 40–7, 55–7, 129
physiotherapists 18, 121–3, 129
placebo 134, 136
practitioner, general 8, 57
prana 135–6
prayer 3, 59, 112, 119
pregnancy 25–7, 33, 64
presence, physical 3, 24, 58,
    121, 124
priests, parish x, 57–9
privacy 12, 25, 43, 45
procedures, medical 40–3
    nursing 40, 44–51, 68–84
    surgical 40, 52
profession, medical x, 18, 45
    nursing x, 18, 45
proxemics 11
psychiatric nursing 97–9
psychiatrist 94–104
psychoanalysis 33, 90
psychogeriatric 98
psychologist 31, 34–6
psychology, dynamic 31, 90
psychotherapy 89–104
psychosis 93, 110

puberty 36
pulse-taking 56–7, 78–82
punishment 35–6

radiations 132–4
radiotherapy 122
rapport 16, 46–7, 91–2
rats 15–16
recovery room 43–4
regression 28–9, 40, 98, 120
relationships, inter-personal x,
    3, 7, 17–18, 40, 47–8, 91,
    109, 121
    mother-child 25–37
religion 6–9
respirators 72–84

sacrifice 137–8
schizophrenia 27, 98–9
scrofula 130–2
security 9, 31, 40–4, 120, 124,
    145
self-acceptance 91
self-disclosure 8, 91–6
self-esteem 25, 42, 109
self-exploration 91
self-identity 43
self-image 110–11
sex 8–9, 13–14, 36, 44, 49, 90,
    92, 101–3, 116, 120, 125
sexuality 8–9, 101
shock 55, 83–4
sickness 40–59
sick-room 41–2
sight 31, 59
silence 10
skin 5, 13, 18–19, 24–6, 29, 33,
    78
skin hunger 120
smell 18
solidarity 18, 59
sound 18, 31
space 11, 42–4, 54
speech 9–10, 29
sport 36

staff, hospital 18, 24, 40–59
stethoscope 56
stimulation, tactile 4, 6, 24,
    65–6, 69
stress 13, 16, 40, 48, 52, 63–84,
    96, 102, 135
stroking 9, 13, 17, 29, 48, 53,
    66–71, 80, 89, 119, 121
sucking 23, 27, 30–1
suffering 41
suggestion 132
surgery 43, 52, 54, 66, 115–31
symbol 123
system, nervous 14

taboo 7–9, 49, 90, 94, 125
tact 6
taste 18
temperament 31
tension 16, 43, 58, 102, 122
terminal illness x, 13, 112–23
territory 11, 43
texture 15
therapist 90, 92–3, 96, 99–103
therapy 92–4, 99, 104
therapy, occupational 14, 46
    physical 14, 46
    speech 14
tie-sign 11
touch, active 4, 31
    affective 111
    caring 35, 46–7, 116–17
    comforting 46–7, 77–8
    exploitative 35, 44, 92
    expressive 46, 102
    grasping 19, 110
    healing 129–41
    instrumental 46–7
    maternal 23–37
    passive 4
    patronising 102
    perfunctory 46–7, 77–8
    reassuring 77–8

related 102
royal 129–32
self 36–7
sensory 36
sexual 91
status 18
supportive 102
sweeping 19
task-related 47, 78–84
therapeutic 54, 134–6
three-dimensional 19
visual 36
transference 90, 92
trauma 55, 93–5
trust 10, 55, 58, 95

unconscious 13, 53, 74–5,
    78–80, 89, 118
unction, holy 140
understanding 53–4, 93, 126
unit, coronary care 77–84
    intensive care 25, 73–7
    neonatal 25, 66–73
    special care baby 66–73
uterus 66

ventilator 68–83
visitors 117–18
visitors, health 19
vulnerability 41–4

well-being 141
wheelchairs 110
wholeness 141
widows 125–6
withdrawal 28
womb 23
workers, health 13, 44
    social x, 44

zones, distance 5, 11
    erogenous 4